GW00537796

ALL SHE LOST

Praise for *All She Lost*:

'*All She Lost* is a courageous and essential piece of journalism. It is a documentation of one of the most scandalous disasters of this century so far, including the corruption and negligence of Lebanon's leadership, and the human stories of those most affected by grave wrongdoing, for which there has still been no justice. Mawad approached this book in a unique way: through interviews with only women and girls, but of every age and background. She is honest about her own emotions throughout and her connection to the crisis, while being thorough with her reporting. I've never seen recent history written like this before and I hugely admire it.'

Sally Hayden, author of *My Fourth Time,
We Drowned* and journalist for the *Irish Times*

'A poignant and compelling account of the collapse of a state. By putting the voices of women at the centre, Dalal Mawad has found a way of telling the tragic story of the Beirut blast and the failure of the Lebanese political class that will resonate with anyone who cares about justice and the abuse of power.'

Lindsey Hilsum, Channel 4 News International Editor
and author of *Sandstorm*

'In her essential and urgent book, Dalal Mawad bears testament to the collapse of Lebanon. Told through the voices of courageous women, this oral history is also warning to all nations that let impunity seep through their foundations.'

Kim Ghattas, journalist and author of *Black Wave*

'*All She Lost* gives voice not just to the women who endured Lebanon's catastrophic port explosion but reveals the burden they have carried for years. Their testimony is heartbreaking and horrifying, each story uniquely shocking. An important account by women of their country's decline and collapse.'

Quentin Sommerville, BBC Middle East Correspondent

'The hitherto untold stories of women in Lebanon expose the crisis-hit country's story of trauma upon trauma without respite. In this sensitive and striking collective memoir, Dalal Mawad gives a voice to those who bear the brunt of the economic and political implosion characterising their homeland's modern collapse.'

Anoosh Chakelian, Britain Editor of The New Statesman

'A painful but necessary book that recounts, with both great compassion and artistry, yet another fatal episode of Lebanon's serial tragedies. No one has told HERstory better and deeper than Dalal Mawad.'

Joumana Haddad, author of *I Killed Scheherazade*

'A beautiful new voice for the unheard.'

Janine di Giovanni, journalist and author
of *The Morning They Came For Us*

'A deeply important, compelling and moving account of a dark moment in Lebanon's history, beautifully told through gripping personal stories of Lebanese women. Dalal Mawad does not just tell the story of Lebanon, but the story of women and the Middle East.'

Ramita Navai, journalist and author of *City of Lies*

'This is a deeply reported and powerful account on the collapse of a country. The testimony that Lebanese journalist Dalal Mawad has gathered is remarkable - and her empathy for all the woman she interviewed shines through on every page. This is a book that will stay with me long after I finished reading it.'

Martin Patience, Senior Producer at NPR

'Dalal Mawad's book on Lebanon is deeply personal – as a little girl, she was swept up in her country's turmoil and later, as a journalist she covered a succession of cataclysmic events. While her own painful experiences vividly frame her writing, it is the astonishing accounts of the women she features that illuminate Lebanon's dark history with their struggle for justice and dignity. An emotionally gripping and enlightening journey.'

Melissa Fleming, the United Nations Under-Secretary-General for Global Communications, and
author of *A Hope More Powerful than the Sea*

ALL SHE LOST

The Explosion in Lebanon, the Collapse
of a Nation and the Women who Survive

DALAL MAWAD

BLOOMSBURY CONTINUUM
LONDON · OXFORD · NEW YORK · NEW DELHI · SYDNEY

BLOOMSBURY CONTINUUM
Bloomsbury Publishing Plc
50 Bedford Square, London, WC1B 3DP, UK
29 Earlsfort Terrace, Dublin 2, Ireland

BLOOMSBURY, BLOOMSBURY CONTINUUM and the Diana logo are trademarks
of Bloomsbury Publishing Plc

First published in Great Britain 2023

A catalogue record for this book is available from the British Library

Library of Congress Cataloging-in-Publication data has been applied for

ISBN: HB: 978-1-3994-0625-3; eBook: 978-1-3994-0621-5; ePDF: 978-1-3994-0622-2

2 4 6 8 10 9 7 5 3 1

Typeset by Deanta Global Publishing Services, Chennai, India
Printed and bound in Great Britain by CPI Group (UK) Ltd, Croydon CRO 4YY

To find out more about our authors and books visit www.bloomsbury.com
and sign up for our newsletters

For my late grandmother Dalal who suffered in silence.

For my daughter Yasma, may you find the peace we never had.

Contents

Map of east Beirut

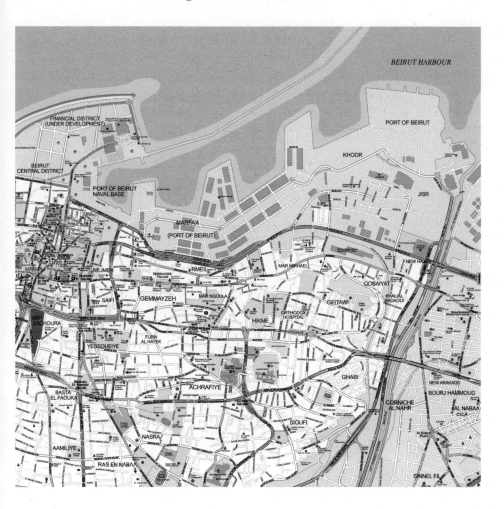

Introduction

Most Lebanese have a story to tell about the explosion in Beirut on 4 August 2020; some are just more painful than others. I was lucky that day – I was not physically hurt. But part of my soul was broken and my life changed forever. A few months later, I moved to France seeking a safer and better future for my daughter who was four years old back then. The fear and anxiety that she experienced brought back my own uncomfortable childhood memories of the endless violence in my country. I do not want her to live that same life. I could not allow that to happen again. I left behind my husband who could not move with us, my entire family, and a country which, despite everything it has taken from me, I will always call home.

The date of 4 August was apocalyptic even by the standards of a nation that has witnessed so much violence and tragedy in the past. On that ill-fated day, a fire ignited in a storage warehouse in the port of Beirut, causing a massive explosion with the force equivalent to 'one-20th of the atomic bomb dropped on Hiroshima'. It was one of the largest non-nuclear explosions ever recorded in history. Extraordinarily, the final, official death toll has still not been published. The Lebanese government stopped counting a month after the blast, putting the toll at 191, but it is believed that at least 221 people were killed and more than 6,000 were injured. The unprecedented magnitude of the physical destruction of the city makes the casualty figure almost seem small by comparison. Many more could have died. Indeed, many of us are only alive through sheer luck. For me, surviving also carried the burden of guilt, the guilt of being alive while so many are gone, the pain of realizing what we lost that day.

I grew up in Lebanon, a small and scenic country in the Middle East, bordering Syria to the north and east, Israel and the occupied Palestinian territories to the south, and the Mediterranean Sea to the west. The modern nation as we know it was born in 1920. But Lebanon had existed for many centuries before, under different political entities and with different borders. It is mentioned in the Bible many times, both in the Old Testament and the New Testament. Its land has been occupied and marked by numerous civilizations, including the Phoenicians, Babylonians, Greeks, Romans, Arabs, and Ottomans, among others.

My youth in Lebanon was often interrupted by violence and conflict. I was born in 1985, five years before the Lebanese civil war ended, so my memory of that period is faint. But there are other dates that I can never forget. In 1996, Israel, which has been in a state of war with Lebanon since its creation in 1948, launched its 'Grapes of Wrath' operation in the south of Lebanon. We had to miss out on school, as classrooms around the country were turned into shelters for those displaced by the aggression. One day, I saw the bodies of children on the news, after what would be known as the Qana massacre. Israel had shelled a United Nations compound holding displaced people, killing 106. I was consumed with fear. I was only 11 and I had mistakenly seen the footage on TV as my parents were watching the news. I slept on my mother's lap that night, crying and throwing up.

Then in 2000, a man who had worked for us fired a gun near my bedroom window after my father had just been elected as a member of parliament. No one is injured but the episode traumatized me. I was only a teenager.

On 14 February 2005 the former prime minister, Rafik Hariri, a critic of Syria's post-war occupation of Lebanon, was killed in a bombing in Beirut along with 21 other civilians near the university campus where I was studying for my undergraduate degree. The explosion happened on the road I took every single day to go home. We took to the streets that year as students demanded truth and justice for his assassination and the end of the Syrian occupation of Lebanon which had been ongoing since 1976. On 14 March 2005 over a million protesters flocked to Beirut demanding the withdrawal of Syria's boots on the ground.

In July 2006, Israel launched another war on Lebanon, and we would live through the traumatizing sounds of airstrikes for almost a month. At least 1,100 Lebanese died and the instability would continue. On 7 May 2008 the Iranian-backed Lebanese Shia militant group Hezbollah, believed to have the largest weapons arsenal in the world for a non-state actor, took up arms against other Lebanese political groups, bringing civil war-like scenes back to the streets of Beirut. Then, in 2013 and 2014, as a journalist, I reported on a series of suicide blasts that rocked the Beirut suburbs and Tripoli, Lebanon's second-largest city. In 2015 and 2019 I covered massive protests that often ended with violence and tear gas. These are just some of the many traumatizing events that have robbed the Lebanese people of any sense of security and that have shaped the woman I am today.

August 4 2020 was just another extremely hot and humid summer day. I was stuck at home behind my computer, working remotely because of the Covid-19 pandemic. I was at the mercy of an unreliable internet connection and enduring, like most Lebanese, the scorching heat and recurrent power cuts. Lebanon's power outages date back to the civil war and have still not been resolved to this day because of corruption.

I was finishing my afternoon shift as a senior producer and correspondent for the Associated Press, covering Lebanon and the wider Middle East region. Lebanon had, like most of the world, been trying to contain the pandemic. But, unlike elsewhere, the virus had hit at a time when the country was already grappling with an unparalleled economic and financial crisis. The economic crash started in 2019, though it originated decades earlier, and then got worse after nationwide protests over a tax increase toppled the government and created an uprising.

Lebanon was soon overtaken by nationwide protests against the ruling political elite. The country was increasingly looking like a failed state. The Lebanese pound had lost more than 80 per cent of its value that summer on the parallel market, more than 95 per cent by the time this book was written, while depositors were denied access to their savings which had actually become worthless. This was the result of a Ponzi (pyramid) scheme, operated by the commercial banks and the political establishment, and in which everyone's money, including mine, vanished overnight. Inflation was soaring rapidly; unemployment and poverty reached new heights, and the collapse of the health sector was a real possibility as hospitals struggled to stay afloat. Covid-19 cases were increasing again, and medical personnel were warning of an imminent disaster. Many, including me, thought the country had hit rock-bottom. Yet, little did we know that a disaster of another kind was waiting around the corner.

My house is about 11 kilometres from Beirut, nestled on a residential hill that overlooks a small and peaceful pine wood. Beirut and its surroundings had become a stifling concrete jungle and I was feeling lucky to have trees to look at and access to some outdoor space during the long summer days of confinement. I had no plans to go to Beirut that day. At about 6:07 p.m. I went to the kitchen to feed my cat, which was waiting for me outside in the garden. It was our ritual every day. As I opened the window and emptied the canned food into a bowl, I heard the familiar roar of warplanes racing through our skies. Israeli warplanes have been violating Lebanese airspace for decades. The jet fighters were exceptionally frequent that summer.

A minute later, at 6:08 p.m., a loud explosion rocked the house, the loudest I had ever heard in my entire life. It sent my cat into hiding and left me in a state of shock. My first thought was that there had been an airstrike nearby. I started shouting helplessly 'They hit us, they hit us!' I rushed inside, desperate to find out if everyone, including my husband and child, were safe. My daughter was with my sister-in-law and was fine. But I couldn't get hold of my husband, who was driving back home at the time. He later made it home safe.

I started looking for information on social media. '6:10 p.m. Was that an airstrike? What was that?' I tweeted. I turned the TV on and unconfirmed reports said there might have been an explosion at the house of the Lebanese prime minister, Saad Hariri, son of Rafik Hariri who was killed in the car bomb attack in 2005.

I tried calling colleagues in Beirut but to no avail. My calls did not go through.

Local media was now reporting that the blast, which was felt miles away in neighbouring Cyprus, was an explosion at the port caused by fireworks in a warehouse. Ten minutes later, one of my colleagues called back. She was hysterical – her roof had collapsed and, though she was miraculously unhurt, her house was badly damaged and she was effectively homeless. I couldn't understand how an explosion at the port had devastated her home several kilometres away. It was very confusing. The first images from the port and the blast started coming in through local TV. I still thought the main impact was at the port itself. Few facts were clear that night. It would take me, and the entire country, until the next morning to realize the magnitude of what had happened.

I drove to Beirut at 6 a.m. for a live broadcast for *Good Morning Britain* from a position near the port. Before I even got to the city, I saw windows and doors blown out miles away from the explosion's epicentre. The destruction had started many kilometres before you entered the capital.

The blast site itself had an eerie tranquillity, the gracious morning light cutting through the smoke that was still billowing above the seaport, its brightness exposing with a piercing clarity the enormity of the destruction. The harbour had been smashed, its tall grain silos stood defeated, one side almost completely collapsed, the other relatively untouched, looking feebly at the devastated city. I drove along the adjacent highway in utter disbelief – the damage was like nothing I had ever seen before. It reminded me of Homs and Aleppo in Syria and Mosul in Iraq, devastated by months of airstrikes, where I had covered the displacement crisis for the United Nations.

Nearly half of Beirut was damaged. My city, which despite previous bouts of violence has remained a haven for artists and activists in the Middle East, and was once a centre of cultural renaissance and creativity, boasting museums, galleries and a history of more than 5,000 years, was devastated.

Three hundred thousand residents had been made homeless overnight, many were injured and left wandering helplessly for a shelter, for help. The destruction was the greatest in the eastern parts of the city. Buildings were battered, naked concrete columns were all that was left of the luxurious skyscrapers overlooking the port. Cars along the road looked like they had been hit by a giant hammer, and streets were blocked by rubble and wreckage. Survivors were already cleaning up the streets, salvaging what they could, looking for survivors. I did not see any police or army officers helping them. As I approached the inner eastern side of the city, the silence was pierced by the sounds of broken glass. This shattering noise became the soundtrack to our lives. It was all we could hear, all day, for many weeks.

For weeks afterwards, I reported around the clock on the blast, both in the field, where I was interviewing people and going live on TV around the world, and from the ruined Associated Press office, producing videos and writing stories. Working in a building where most of the windows were smashed, and the ceiling and some of the walls had collapsed, was quite a challenge. Had we not been working from home at the time of the explosion because of the pandemic, my colleagues and I would very likely have been hurt or even killed. For days, I had a recurring nightmare about dragging a bleeding colleague out of the office. Even before the explosion, I suffered from post-traumatic stress disorder (PTSD) as a result of all the trauma I had witnessed in my life in the Middle East. Any distress sends me back into a vicious cycle of anxiety and night terrors.

In the days after 4 August, I kept hearing about relatives who had been injured and friends who had died. My mother's friend, my cousin's childhood best friend, my relative's husband, a friend's daughter, all dead. My sister was injured, both of my aunts were also hurt, their homes were damaged, my colleagues were rendered homeless. This was no longer just another event I would report on; it would become the most painful and personal story I would tell in my decade-long career as a journalist.

Many of the stories I wrote about focused on the psychological toll of the blast. In Lebanon, new traumas pile on top of previous ones before you've had time to recover. People who survived the explosion were also survivors of the 2019 economic crisis, the survivors of the many wars with Israel, survivors of the civil war, the political assassinations, and the endless cycles of Lebanon's violence.

I began putting together survivors' stories, particularly from women, although that was never a deliberate choice at the outset. Many of these women lost everything that day: the most precious people in their lives, their physical and mental health, their homes and livelihoods, their ability to be happy and to feel in any way secure.

Mothers who lost their children in the explosion, wives who lost their partners, doctors and nurses, first-aid responders, refugees, and migrants – each recalled the moment at 6:08 p.m., sharing the story of their loss and the harrowing details carved into their memories of the day that changed their lives.

These women's homes turned into a front line on 4 August. The most secure place in their lives was no longer safe.

But the more I listened to them, the more I realized it wasn't just that they had witnessed an apocalyptic moment. Their losses went way beyond the blast. They tell the story of Lebanon's modern collapse and their life as women in it, often characterized by violence, oppression, and discrimination, but also by survival and extraordinary endurance. This book is a collective memoir of my country's recent history narrated by its marginalized women.

Women in Lebanon have been historically at the foreground of the struggle for social and political rights. Women marched in 1943 ahead of independence from France that year. They took up arms in the civil war, resisted and mediated for peace, then organized in movements to rebuild Lebanon. They have played an important but underestimated role in the history of the country.

The 2019 uprising emboldened and empowered women like never before. A video of a woman kicking a politician's security guard who tried to attack her helped galvanize the onset of what became known as the October movement. In every protest, women formed protective barriers between the police and the demonstrators. They were at the heart of public debates and new political movements. Despite this, little progress on women's rights has been achieved since. In the 2022 parliamentary elections, short of a women's quota, only 113 women ran for office out of a total 1,043 candidates, and only eight were elected for the 128-seat parliament, most of them affiliated with the traditional political parties. Women only represent 23 per cent of the workforce in Lebanon and are still denied many rights.

Feminist movements in Lebanon are increasingly vocal. Women-led groups have for the past few years advocated for parity between the sexes and amendments to the law, but they have scored only minor victories. In fact, the reality remains grim.

Lebanon's laws largely discriminate against women. For instance, to this day, women married to foreigners can't pass on their nationality to their children. Women's personal-status laws around family relations – such as marriage, divorce, inheritance, and custody – are not covered under a unified civil code but are defined and managed by the courts of the different independent religious communities, courts which not only discriminate against women but also treat them unequally depending on their sect. A Catholic woman, for example, does not have the same rights as an Orthodox woman or a Muslim Sunni woman, and a Muslim Sunni woman doesn't have the same rights as a Muslim Shia woman. One example is child custody. In divorce cases, Shia women only have custody of boys until age two and of girls until seven; Sunni women have custody of both boys and girls until age 12; Greek Orthodox women have custody of boys until 14 and of girls until 15; while Catholic women only have custody of children until age two. The list goes on and on with different rules for different sects.

In the aftermath of the explosion many of the women survivors had legal obstacles to overcome on top of the emotional ones. For example, Catholic Maronite widows with children needed a male custodian from their spouse's family and could not proceed with any decisions regarding the children. This included benefiting from any inheritance, indemnities or reparations without a civil court order every time money was cashed in. Some of the women I spoke to are also survivors of domestic violence, with little protection under the law. They may suffer for years at the hands of abusive husbands, and those who make it through alive are then faced with the herculean effort required to seek a divorce in the religious courts. Lebanon passed an imperfect law in 2014 aiming to protect women from marital violence; it had many flaws, including not protecting women from marital rape. The law, like most in the country, is still not widely implemented. Many of the men accused of abuse still find protection from their political groups and escape accountability.

Justice in Lebanon remains hostage to politicians' interference and misogynistic religious courts. One of the women I interviewed, whose daughter died in the blast, was still fighting in a Muslim

Sunni religious court to prevent her abusive former husband from benefiting from the trickle of state repatriations dispensed to families of the victims. Another survivor was fighting a battle in a Muslim Shia court to have custody of her son after his father took him away from her while she was in a coma following the blast.

Foreign women, mainly migrant workers, face another layer of discrimination. They suffer years of abuse, often violence, due to labour laws for foreigners that have been described as a form of modern slavery.

Many of these women suffer silently. They never get the chance to heal or find justice. In many ways the women in this book remind me of my own paternal grandmother. She lost her husband in the reprisals that followed a massacre during a politicized family feud in my home town of Zgharta in 1957. During a requiem mass in the village of Miziara near Zgharta, family clans fighting over personal and political issues killed each other. More than 30 died that day.

My grandfather, who was a pharmacist and had nothing to do with politics, was shot in his pharmacy by a man from a rival family clan. He was a victim of the revenge killings that ensued. The Miziara massacre of 1957 is considered by many as a rehearsal for the wider divisions that would trigger Lebanon's civil wars as early as 1958.

The man who killed my grandfather was held in custody briefly. He served just a short prison sentence before being set free following some political interference. My grandmother had to fight the pain and injustice alone, raise two kids alone, and survive the civil war alone. She sacrificed her life for her kids, to meet the expectations of others. She never spoke publicly of the violence that was inflicted upon her, rarely protested her pain, and and never tried to challenge the role expected of her.

Despite all her hardship, she was a cocoon of love and sensitivity who raised two bright boys and helped raise her seven grandchildren. Her boys were her pride and joy, and they both ended up being successful doctors and contributors to their communities. But my grandmother was miserable most of the time – at least that is how I remember her. She often struggled quietly and died a bitter woman, denied the right to live, to love, to seek justice, to heal and start anew.

I grew up surrounded by women like her, women who were caught again and again in vicious cycles of violence and marginalization. The violence of war, sexual violence, and recently economic violence.

Few women have the opportunity to speak out, to talk about that violence, and the pain that lingers year after year. I on the other hand have been privileged throughout my life. I have successfully fought to be heard and to stand out. What use is my voice, though; unless these women can also be heard?

Women opened up to me, even months after the explosion. Many of them were speaking about the blast for the first time, trusting me with their pain, sharing their powerful and very personal stories. Few women refused to be interviewed – and those who did told me it was simply because they just weren't capable of going back to that painful event. At times I felt like a therapist, listening for uninterrupted hours to these heart-wrenching accounts. Most of the women cried every time we spoke. So did I. It was overwhelming, to say the least, to sit there, sometimes in homes that had been turned into giant memorials with the victims' pictures all around. I also felt helpless not being able to do much for them. This is exactly how I felt when, as a young kid, sitting alone with my grandmother, she would tell me about my grandfather's murder and start to cry. I sat there, in pain, but completely powerless.

I met most of these women in the intimate setting of their homes. They opened their door to me with no conditions, they welcomed me as if we already knew each other. I interviewed dozens of them, young and old, Lebanese and foreigners, from different backgrounds. For editorial reasons, not all of them made it into this book. But all of their accounts were powerful and heartbreaking. All I did was ask general questions about the fateful day of 4 August and then let them direct me, take me to the places they wanted to go back to, to the stories they wanted to tell. I recorded and transcribed the interviews verbatim, and then added context about the issues they mentioned and my own experience. This book is the result.

Lebanon's women have rarely written about their history although they were major players in it. Their past, present, and future have all been held hostage to decisions taken by men. This is why a women-led narrative is now more important than ever.

The women in this book all experienced the explosion and suffered unimaginable loss and tragedy, but it is not just this one event that brings them together. Their personal stories converged to tell the story of a nation whose glory days are long gone, now riven by protracted violence, lurching from crisis to crisis, and fighting to survive. These women have witnessed the ultimate blow to Lebanon, embodied in the tragic blast of 4 August.

They are also victims of Lebanon's modern history of protracted conflicts and prolonged trauma. They have been forced to be resilient but are in reality just survivors of the country's perpetual dysfunction and now its economic and financial collapse. Before the crisis, less than 30 per cent of Lebanon's population were considered poor. As this book is being written, more than 80 per cent of its population are now living below the poverty line, 36 per cent of them in extreme poverty. The devaluation of the pound means that most people can't access basic goods, medical care, and education. The country is also literally drowning in darkness. Because of the shortage of fuel, blackouts can last for up to 23 hours a day.

Three years since the onset of the economic crisis of 2019, the political elite has not implemented any structural changes. The International Monetary Fund pledged to give Lebanon 3 billion dollars on condition of economic reforms, including formal capital control, a unified exchange rate, a reformed bank secrecy law, among other things. As of the end of 2022, none of these conditions had been carried out.

Most importantly, these women and their struggles embody Lebanon's endless uphill battle for truth and justice, both evasive. All these women are fighting for accountability that unfortunately seems impossible. They are also fighting for a nation that was once envied by its neighbours and is now at the bottom of the abyss, a nation agonizingly losing its talent and struggling to stay alive.

The book tells not only of what these women have lost, but also what Beirut has lost, the Lebanon that is no more.

WHAT WE KNOW

On 4 August 2020 a fire erupted around 5:35 p.m. in Beirut's port, according to eyewitness accounts. But surprisingly it was not reported to the Beirut firefighters' brigade until 5:54 p.m. According to Lieutenant Ali Najm, who heads public relations at the brigade, four consecutive calls were made to his unit around that time, one by the police, another by General Security, and then two by individuals working at the port. They all reported a fire at the port, without any further details. Ten firefighters – nine men and one woman – raced to the harbour, some in a truck and others in an ambulance, not knowing that they were heading towards their inevitable death.

In the meantime, people watched curiously from their homes as the growing smoke billowed into the sky. Many stood by windows, on rooftops and balconies, filming the scene with their mobile phones, unaware that what would happen next would be one of the largest non-nuclear explosions in history.

According to Najm, the fire started in warehouse 12, and the firefighters reported that it was locked. They tried to break into it but failed. After they saw the magnitude of the fire, the firefighters called for additional support. They had no idea what was in the warehouse nor what was burning. They couldn't get inside.

As more firefighters got ready to head to the port at 6:08 p.m., Beirut was shaken by twin blasts. The strength of the second one tore through the city, sending people flying, slashing them with shattered glass. None of the firefighters at the port made it out alive.

The explosion was caused by a consignment of ammonium nitrate, according to Lebanese officials, which had been stored in Beirut's port for years but whose origin and destination remain a mystery to this day. It killed at least 221 people and injured approximately 6,000, many of them critically.

The victims were not just Lebanese. They included nationals from Syria, Egypt, Ethiopia, Bangladesh, the Philippines, Pakistan, Palestine, the Netherlands, Canada, Germany, France, Australia, and the United States. Even in a country that has seen more than its fair share of conflict, never have so many people in Lebanon experienced the same traumatizing event at the same time.

The explosion is the result of both the criminal and corrupt manoeuvring of the ruling political establishment, especially because the Port of Beirut's management structure reflects the division of power among the ruling elite. It is very much a microcosm of the corruption in Lebanon as a whole.

Many of Lebanon's current political leaders were warlords in the country's civil war, a complicated multifaceted conflict that erupted in 1975 and lasted until 1990. These leaders have been governing the country since then. They head political parties that are sectarian in nature and they consider themselves the patrons, or *Zu'amas* in Arabic, of Lebanon's various sectarian communities. They have benefited from and consolidated a power-sharing system along sectarian lines which includes an official division of seats in parliament between the 18 different religious groups. This power-sharing arrangement is unofficially and tacitly implemented in the make-up of the Cabinet and the appointment of civil servants within state institutions. Moreover, there are effectively three presidents, divided among the three largest sects; the prime minister is a Sunni

Muslim, the president is a Maronite Christian, and the speaker of parliament is a Shia Muslim.

Different sects control different state departments and agencies, and everyone gets a share of the corruption ring. This political power-sharing system has also nurtured a web of clientelism that has made these politicians stronger than the state itself. They control its institutions and use its resources to serve their parochial interests. The Beirut port is no exception.

One powerful and dominant group at the port is the armed Shia militant group Hezbollah, which is backed by Iran and is considered to be stronger than Lebanon's national army, controlling decisions of war and peace, and interfering in regional proxy wars including the one in neighbouring Syria. Hezbollah has fought alongside the Assad regime in Syria since 2013, providing ground support for the Syrian dictator and preventing his military defeat by domestic and foreign forces.

Lebanon has always been wedged in by regional tensions and conflicts. Its political parties have long sought external support to reinforce their internal positions, while foreign powers have used Lebanon as a pawn to advance their regional hegemonic interests.

Lebanon's judiciary, too, is hostage to the interests of the political establishment. Politicians directly interfere in the appointment and promotion of judges, often along sectarian lines. This largely explains the absence of an independent legal system in the country, and the prevalent culture of impunity as a result.

People wonder to this day why explosive chemicals were left in a functioning port in the heart of a city for years. There is still no definite answer. According to media investigations and a Human Rights Watch report released on 3 August 2021, various senior officials, ministers from different political parties, prime ministers, and the Lebanese president were all aware of the presence of hundreds of tons of ammonium nitrate and the danger this posed. But no one took the appropriate action.

Why it was there in the first place is far from the only question that remains to be answered. What ignited the fire in warehouse 12 that day? Was it really an accident? Who owned this lethal cargo? Whose decision was it to store ammonium nitrate for so long in incredibly unsafe conditions? Why, even though authorities knew what was stored at the warehouse, were a dozen doomed firefighters sent to put out a fire caused by its ignition? Why was there no immediate order to evacuate the perimeters around the port, after the fire broke out?

What we do know is that seven years previously, a Moldovan-flagged ship, the MV *Rhosus*, left the port of Batumi in Georgia carrying some 2,750 tons of ammonium nitrate from a factory known as Rusta-vi Azot. The vessel was reportedly heading for an explosives company in Mozambique. The official narrative of the Lebanese authorities was that the ship made an unplanned stop in Beirut on 19 November 2013 to take on additional cargo (heavy seismic equipment borrowed from Lebanon for oil and gas exploration) to be delivered back to Jordan. The ship had been leased and operated by a Russian man named Igor Grechushkin. He reportedly wanted to dock in Beirut to take on the additional cargo, to make more money in order to pay for crossing the Suez Canal – according to the Russian captain, Boris Prokoshev, who was on board the *Rhosus* and spoke to various media outlets. So far, no one has been able to verify this claim.

In its report, Human Rights Watch stated: 'The evidence to date raises questions regarding whether the ammonium nitrate was intended for Mozambique, as the *Rhosus*' shipping documents stated, or whether Beirut was the intended destination.'

This additional cargo, which proved to be extremely heavy, was loaded onto the *Rhosus*, according to port documents, and 'the ship started buckling under the weight of the seismic equipment', according to Aya Majzoub, who was leading the Human Rights

Watch investigation. The *Rhosus* was grounded and never allowed to leave the port.

Its contents were offloaded into warehouse 12 on 23 and 24 October 2014 as the result of a Lebanese judicial order. In February 2018 the *Rhosus* sank in the harbour. But Human Rights Watch says the official narrative doesn't make sense, because it was known from the beginning that the ship could not take on such heavy machinery. 'The ship was already overweight and according to experts it was not the type of boat that could take on such equipment,' added Majzoub. 'So why was it allowed to load it?'

Investigative work by the Lebanese journalist Firas Hatoum has traced the ammonium nitrate cargo back to a shell company registered in the United Kingdom and linked to Syrian–Russian businessmen, George Haswani and Mudalal Khouri, with close ties both to Russia's president Vladimir Putin and the Assad regime. These businessmen had also previously been sanctioned by the United States for aiding the Assad government, including 'attempting to purchase Ammonium Nitrate for Syria in late 2013', according to the US Treasury.

The *Rhosus* itself was initially owned by a Cypriot man, Charalambos Manoli, according to the Organized Crime and Corruption Reporting Project. The report said that at the time, 'Manoli was in debt to a Lebanese-owned bank that lost multiple licenses for alleged money-laundering offenses, including helping the Shia militant group Hezbollah and a company linked to Syria's weapons of mass destruction program.'

Manoli was in the process of selling the ship to Grechushkin, according to the Human Rights Watch investigation, but oddly Grechushkin never made the effort to finalize the purchase once the vessel was held in Beirut's port.

In the summer of 2022 a new investigative documentary by Firas Hatoum found that four vessels coming from Georgia had docked in Beirut and Tripoli, and Tartous in Syria, between 2012 and 2104. According to Hatoum, these ships were part of the 'Odessa Network', a group of businessmen, companies, and ships accused of delivering weapons from Russia and Ukraine to the Assad regime since 2011. Hatoum obtained data showing that Georgia actually exported 44,335 tons of ammonium nitrate between 2012 and 2014, reportedly intended for Mozambique. But data from the World Bank's Integrated Trade Solution website (WITS) showed that Mozambique never imported ammonium nitrate from Georgia. The final intended destination of the ammonium nitrate therefore remains unknown, except for the 2,750 tons which were stored in the port of Beirut and made known to the world after the 4 August explosion.

According to an article by Reuters released in July 2021, an FBI report has stated that only about 500 tons of the ammonium nitrate exploded that day in August. Local reports also showed that before the explosion, the consignment in the warehouse had been mishandled and badly stored, sacks of ammonium nitrate were torn, and lots of powder was scattered on the ground. A report commissioned by the government but only leaked after the explosion showed that the explosive fertilizer had been mishandled, and it questioned how well it was stored and how much of it remained. No one has yet been able to find evidence that this specific cargo was being used or sold by the port authorities, but if not all the ammonium nitrate exploded, then it raises another question: where had the rest gone? Why did it not explode? Was it being exported to Syria from the port of Beirut and warehouse 12? Was ammonium nitrate used in barrel bombs or explosives that were being made in Syria as of 2014?

Various forensic reports, including one by Forensic Architecture, have revealed that the ammonium nitrate was stored with fireworks, various types of oil, acid and other inflammable material. Why would the port authorities have stored all of these dangerous goods without any appropriate protection and safety measures?

During the course of writing this book, these questions have remained unanswered and no one has been held in any way responsible. The political establishment is holding justice hostage.

Human Rights Watch, which has been leading the unofficial efforts to investigate the blast, has been summoned by Hezbollah, according to Majzoub, and told over a cup of coffee with the head of the party's international affairs bureau 'not to waste time' as the 'truth will never see the light', and instead to worry 'about other pressing issues'. In February 2021, intellectual and prominent Hezbollah critic, Lokman Slim, was shot dead in his car in the south of Lebanon, in an area known to be a stronghold of Hezbollah. In one of his last interviews on television, Slim had accused Hezbollah of having ties to the ammonium nitrate that caused the Beirut blast. His family believes his death, and the death of two others, a retired customs officer and a forensic photographer, could be linked to the explosion.

Hezbollah is not the only powerful player at the Beirut port. Other political parties also have authority and have benefited from the corruption in the port operations, including traffic and customs. A few days after the explosion, 25 civil servants, including senior officials at the port with various political affiliations, were arrested. But these public servants, innocent or not, are only at the bottom of the chain of accountability.

In fact, a few months after the blast, Judge Fadi Sawan filed charges against the former prime minister, Hassan Diab, who submitted his resignation six days after the explosion (10 August), and three former ministers, two of whom were lawmakers at the time: Finance Minister Ali Hassan Khalil and former Public Works ministers Youssef Fenianos and Ghazi Zaiter. They were accused of negligence leading to the deaths of so many people, and they were the main accused. But they refused to show up for questioning, claiming 'political immunity rights'. They invoked Article 40 of the Lebanese constitution which states that no member of parliament 'may, during the sessions, be prosecuted or arrested for a criminal offence, without the permission of the Chamber, except when caught in the act'. Judge Sawan was dismissed from his job a few months later by a court order.

Today, the investigation is in the hands of Judge Tarek Bitar. In July 2021 he requested permission from parliament to investigate MPs and high-level security officials about the explosion, including the aforementioned former Finance Minister Ali Hassan Khalil, former Public Works ministers Ghazi Zaiter and Youssef Fenianos, the MP and former Interior Minister Nouhad Machnouk, the head of the General Security Directorate, Major General Abbas Ibrahim, and the head of State Security, Major General Tony Saliba. But once again the claim of 'immunity' was used to turn down the judge's request.

The accused ministers initiated a series of suspension requests to block the prosecution, including removing the lead prosecutor from his post. Judge Bitar was even accused by Hezbollah's leader, Hassan Nasrallah, of bias and asked that he be removed from the probe.

As this book is being written, Judge Bitar, who had been blocked from pursuing his investigation, had unexpectedly returned to work, escalating the opposition of the ruling class against him. He filed new charges in January 2023 against a number of officials including the country's public prosecutor Ghassan Oueidat. Oueidat ordered the unconditional release of all those who had been detained since August 2020 and even filed charges against Bitar. The war between the public prosecutor and the investigating judge might have put the last nail in the coffin of the Lebanese investigation into the blast. Families of the victims want accountability but that has been thwarted by a ruling class desperate to protect itself and is even willing to go after the victims themselves to evade responsibility. Following a protest in front of Beirut's Palace of Justice in January 2023, several relatives of the victims were questioned by the police and accused of rioting. Instead of pursuing the officials who are suspects in the explosion, the authorities went after the families asking for justice. It is surreal.

Many victims' relatives are calling today for an international investigation. Some survivors with dual nationality have been able to take legal action against the government from abroad, while others have submitted a lawsuit against Savaro Limited (the shell company that owned the cargo). In February 2023, the British High Court of Justice ruled that Savaro was liable. It was a first and rare victory for the victims and their families.

In the summer of 2022, some families also filed a lawsuit in Texas against Spectrum Geo, the owner of a company that reportedly sub-chartered the Rhosus ship which carried the highly explosive ammonium nitrate in 2012.

I have not yet made peace with 4 August. I don't know if I ever will. There is a voice in my head which keeps telling me that I could have done more that day. That night I stayed at home as I could not get into Beirut. At that stage I had no idea how big the explosion really was, how much loss and tragedy was out there. I wasn't sent on assignment until the early hours of the following morning. As a journalist, I feel like I failed. As a Lebanese, I also feel like I have failed. As a human, I feel guilty just for being alive.

I have played the scenario in my head over and again. My daughter and mother were on the port road at 6.07 p.m. the night before the blast. It seemed so absurd that not only was I safe, but they were safe too. It is hard to accept. This book, these accounts, might be a way for me to process my own trauma and guilt and better understand that day, but it is mostly an attempt to make peace with it. I feel, as a journalist, I owe it to all these people, to my country, to tell these stories.

Timeline

A BUILD-UP OF LEBANON'S 2019 ECONOMIC CRISIS

1950–1966

Lebanon is a 'merchant republic'. It is seen as a transit route for trade. Its economy is outward-oriented, heavily relies on imports and is largely one of services and banking. Agriculture and industries are marginalized.

The 1950s witness an unparalleled increase in the number of commercial banks.

A banking secrecy law passed in 1956 attracts foreign capital including Palestinian capital and oil money from Arab states.

1959 marks the birth of The Association of Lebanese Banks which becomes, with time, a powerful lobby.

1963–64 sees the establishment of Lebanon's Central Bank. It has a weak supervisory role over commercial banks.

1966–1975

Lebanon's largest financial institution, Intra Bank, crashes as a result of political and financial factors.

Intra's collapse leads to major reforms of the banking sector including tighter financial regulations and a bigger authority for the Central Bank over commercial banks.

1975–1990

A civil war takes place in Lebanon, with far-reaching consequences for the economy.

The Lebanese pound starts depreciating in the early 1980s. In 1987 there is an unprecedented economic crisis, affecting lower-income and middle-income families.

1990–1997

In 1992, following the end of the civil war, Rafik Hariri, a Lebanese-Saudi businessman, becomes Prime Minister.

In 1993, Hariri appoints his personal account manager at Merrill Lynch, Riad Salameh, as governor of the Central Bank.

Salameh starts a policy of gradually stabilizing the Lebanese pound.

Lebanon witnesses post-civil war growth, mainly driven by reconstruction and real-estate development, especially in downtown Beirut.

Hariri bets on peace in Lebanon and the region.

Much of the reconstruction is financed through borrowing, mostly from local banks at high interest rates.

Lebanon starts accruing public debt, internal and external. The balance of trade is continuously in deficit and leaking foreign exchange reserves.

It is also the beginning of post-war levels of corruption spearheaded by the political elite and Syria's occupation of Lebanon.

1997–2007

In 1997 the Lebanese pound is pegged to the dollar at a rate of 1,500 pounds to the dollar. The peg proves expensive, depleting foreign-exchange reserves.

The lira is overpriced. Lebanon is a highly dollarized economy that relies largely on imports.

To keep the currency peg, and fund its current account deficit, Lebanon issues Eurobonds, relies on tourism, Arab countries' deposits in Lebanese banks, foreign direct investments (FDIs), and foreign aid.

The banking sector is also greatly dependent on Lebanese remittances from abroad.

In 2001 and then in 2002, Lebanon gets support from the international community through the Paris I and Paris II donors conference. It buys time to maintain its solvency and stay afloat but fails to implement much-needed public-sector reforms.

2007–2011

The destructive Israeli–Lebanese war of 2006 is followed by international money flowing in to Lebanon.

A Paris III conference in 2007 pledges $7.6 billion in support of Lebanon; nearly half is disbursed. Lebanon buys time and liquidity once again.

In 2008, and despite political stalemate in the country, Lebanon benefits from capital inflows following the global economic crisis.

The economy shows excellent growth between 2007 and 2009, with GDP growing by 9 to 10 per cent.

2011–2016

Growth slows down.

Lebanon witnesses a massive influx of Syrian refugees.

Foreign currency inflows are reduced mainly because of regional turmoil and the war in neighbouring Syria. Lebanese remittances decline.

Gulf countries ban their citizens from visiting Lebanon. Tourism declines and foreign direct investment retreats.

2016–2019

The country's debt to GDP ratio stands at more than 150 per cent, the third highest in the world.

Interest payments consume more than half of the state revenues. In 2016 the central bank orchestrates a Ponzi scheme to finance the state's growing twin deficits and to maintain the peg. Commercial banks are accomplices in the scheme. Depositors are lured by high interest rates reaching 20 per cent in some banks.

A public-sector pay rise in 2017, right before parliamentary elections, becomes the straw that breaks the camel's back.

2019–2020

In October 2019 the government increases taxes, including on WhatsApp calls, in an attempt to increase its dwindling revenues.

Mass protests ensue around the country. Banks, already suffering losses, shut down for two weeks. People rush to take out their deposits and savings as soon as the banks reopen. Banks impose informal capital controls. Depositors' money is mere ink on paper.

In March 2020 the Covid-19 pandemic hits the country that is already in crisis, further exacerbating the economic fallout. The government defaults on its foreign debt for the first time in history.

By the summer of 2020, the currency has lost more than 80 per cent of its value on the so-called 'parallel market'. Inflation skyrockets. Fuel and medicines are in short supply.

On 4 August 2020, Beirut is devastated by an explosion at the port. At least 220 are killed, and more than 6000 injured. The damage to the economy is estimated at more than $8 billion by the World Bank.

PART ONE

The Ultimate Blow

In the autumn of 2019, Lebanon enters an unprecedent chapter of its history. The country slides into a downward spiral of economic shocks, experiencing one of the worst global economic crises in the last 150 years.

The political economy of Lebanon has been influenced over the years both by bad governance and regional political developments. The unprecedented economic crisis was caused by years of structural problems and corruption, but was also deepened by regional political instability.

On the eve of 4 August 2020 the Lebanese were struggling with a pandemic, a collapsed currency, soaring inflation, and growing economic uncertainty. The explosion at Beirut's port marked the ultimate blow for the 100-year-old Middle Eastern nation.

Lebanon would never be the same again.

'Nationwide protests paralyzed Lebanon on Friday as thousands of demonstrators blocked major roads in a second day of rallies against the government's handling of a severe economic crisis and the country's political class they perceive as being corrupt.'
18 October 2019, Associated Press

'Lebanon's prime minister, Saad Hariri, has announced his resignation, in a move set to spark further uncertainty in a country paralyzed by political dysfunction and nationwide protests.'
29 October 2019, the Guardian

2

'Banks have been intermittently closed since
mid-October and depositors across the country
are finding it impossible to gain access to
dollar balances.'
22 December 2019, the Financial Times

'Lebanon announces formation of new government.
Protests continue despite breakthrough, as
demonstrators call for early elections and
technocrat-led cabinet.'
22 January 2020, Al Jazeera

'Lebanese are buying candles in bulk, turning to
traditional kerosene lamps and throwing away
rotten food because of prolonged power cuts that
plunged the country into darkness this week, adding
to the gloom of a deepening economic crisis.'
7 July 2020, Associated Press

'Lebanese hospitals, long considered among the
best in the Middle East, are letting go of staff,
reporting shortages in vital medical supplies and
pouring money into fuel for generators because
of power cuts.'
22 July 2020, Associated Press

'Lebanon's financial crisis, rooted in decades of state
corruption and waste, marks the biggest threat to
the country's stability since the 1975–90 civil war.
A collapsing currency has led to soaring inflation
and poverty, and savers have lost free access to
accounts in a paralyzed banking system.'
3 August 2020, France 24

I

The Blast

RITA BADAOUI

*'In my mind, blood is not cold. I asked my
colleague if we were dead. Maybe this is
what death feels like.'*

The afternoon of 4 August 2020 was not busy for the 31-year-old doctor. Rita was in her last year as a cardiology fellow at Saint George Hospital University Medical Centre in Beirut, one of Lebanon's oldest and most renowned private medical teaching centres. The hospital, less than 2 kilometres away from the capital's port, was already reeling under the burden of the country's unprecedented economic crisis. 'Insurance companies were no longer paying money, and people were not coming in like before,' Rita told me in her apartment outside Beirut, which was not too far from where I lived.

The Covid-19 pandemic had hit the country at a time when it was already in crisis. By the summer of 2020, Lebanon's currency, once pegged to the dollar, had lost more than 80 per cent of its value. Banks restricted people's ability to withdraw from their dollar deposits or pay with credit cards. Those with savings in dollars could not take them out and those who had revenues and deposits in Lebanese pounds saw their purchasing power reduced. Many Lebanese could no longer afford healthcare, especially in private medical centres. Lebanon's hospitals, once among the best in the Middle East, were struggling to pay salaries and import medical supplies because of the devaluation in the Lebanese pound and a shortage of foreign currency.

The American University of Beirut Medical Center, once a prestigious regional hospital, attracting Arabs and foreigners for its quality healthcare services, had laid off hundreds of employees in July 2020. Some hospitals were even shutting down entire departments due to a lack of medical supplies and decades-long power cuts, now exacerbated by a fuel shortage. The Lebanese state, which over the years had accrued budget and trade deficits and a debt to GDP ratio among the highest in the world, owed private hospitals billions of dollars. For the first time in its history, in March 2020, Lebanon defaulted on its foreign debt.

My dad, a surgeon and oncologist, who owns and manages a hospital in the north of Lebanon, has had to shut down up to 50 per cent of his wards since the onset of the crisis. The government owes him millions of dollars for patients he took in and who were insured by the state, but never paid their bills.

Public hospitals, underfunded, were also threatened with closure that summer, especially the ones leading the fight against the pandemic.

Rita finished her shift at Saint George Hospital at 5:00 p.m. on Tuesday 4 August. 'I could have gone home,' she said, 'but it was very hot and there was a lot of traffic that day because they [the government] had interrupted the lockdown.'

The government had awkwardly decided to enforce a two-day lockdown to combat rising cases of Covid-19 on 4 and 5 August. And so, Rita decided to stay late to avoid the rush and do some research at the hospital's library, a room on the ground floor with glass facades overlooking the Beirut port.

'Around 5:35 p.m. I started seeing smoke coming out of the port. It was big and white when it first started. I looked at the other doctors in the room, and we were all wondering what that was. We were wondering what was happening. We went outdoors to the terrace, out of curiosity. The smoke was growing, and we could hear a popping sound, like fireworks. It was a weird noise. That's when I took a video and I sent it on the WhatsApp group of the hospital's residents. I asked if others were seeing anything, maybe from another perspective since I was on a lower floor. They said they could only see smoke.'

Rita said she went back indoors but could not stop looking at the fire as it grew bigger and bigger.

'It started turning grey, then it turned black. I could even see some colours. There were colourful sparks, blue and red. It was already 5:45 p.m.'

That's when she remembered sending a video to her mother, in which she asked her if the fire was being reported on the news. Lebanese, whose country has been rocked with different bouts of violence, are quick to turn to each other and the media with concerns at the smallest sign that disrupts their daily peace.

'She said there wasn't anything. I was in disbelief that no one was reporting this. This wasn't normal, something was happening. When the cloud grew very big and became black, the world turned completely dark. The smoke was everywhere, we couldn't see anything. Everyone got closer to the glass, which is really bad now that I think of it. I remember seeing a huge number of birds flying out of the port and I was wondering why so many birds were taking flight. You won't believe how many. Then, that's when the popping grew louder and I heard a sound that seemed like the roar of a jetfighter. It was really scary. The glass was shaking. I was told that I screamed at everyone to run. I don't remember this part at all. I didn't run away. I froze.

'The world turned completely dark, then it exploded. It was 6:08 p.m.'

Rita said she saw the time on her phone.

'The second explosion, maybe half a minute later or less, shoved me across the floor to the next room behind me, throwing me against the wall.

'I flew. The force of the explosion hurt so much. I was stuck to the wall, couldn't move, and felt all the pressure tearing my body apart. I saw everything around me fly. It lasted for a while, around thirty seconds, because we were close to the port. I couldn't understand what was happening. I could feel something cold running down my face. In my mind, blood is not cold. I asked my colleague if we were dead. Maybe this is what death feels like. I never felt like this before. He told me he didn't know.

'I am not a religious person but I started praying that if there was a God or a third force or whatever, that I would accept to die but I just wanted to be in one piece so that my parents don't suffer when they bury me.'

As Rita was saying this, her mother walked in to greet me, carrying cake and juice. We met at her parents' house in the summer of 2021, where Rita still lived. Many Lebanese young men and women usually wait until they are married to leave their family nest. Many of them also stay to save on rent. That became even more prevalent with the economic crisis.

We waited until her mother retreated.

'There was too much blood on my face. I could barely see. My clothes were torn. I couldn't even recognize the place anymore. The wall was not there anymore.

'There was a chilling silence after the explosion. Not a sound. Nothing. And then, the alarm of the hospital went off. I will never forget the sound. I still hear it every day.'

Her colleague told her to get up and go to the Emergency Room, thinking they would get help there.

'We had to go through a hole in the wall and out to the terrace, then onto the road, holding each other's hands. It was only a few minutes after the blast. We were one of the first ones out. We arrived at the ER and realized we were the first people to get there. There was no ER left really.'

The explosion had completely destroyed Saint George Hospital as well as two other large hospitals close to the port, and had damaged at least twelve other medical facilities in Beirut.

'I will never forget the smell. It was horrible and I felt like my trachea was burning. The sky was orange and we could barely see. As soon as the smoke dissipated, I looked around. The hospital had no windows. There were things flying out of the building. I could hear people screaming, everyone was screaming, and the alarm was still on. I still didn't understand what had happened. Imagine, that I had still not linked the fire that I filmed to the explosion. I didn't think a fire could do that, I was sure someone was bombing us.'

Rita said she spent a few hours after that trying to help colleagues and the injured, completely oblivious to her own condition and injuries. She was badly cut in the head and in her eye, and also had a partially torn ligament in her ankle.

'Patients were now being evacuated down to the parking lot which turned into an ER. But it was not the army or the civil defence who came to bring them down, it was other residents themselves, who were injured, that helped them. I didn't see anyone come to the rescue except the Red Cross. It took hours to evacuate people in ambulances to other hospitals.'

Rita's account of the absence of authorities in the aftermath of the blast was one that I heard from dozens of people I interviewed. Aside from Red Cross volunteers, it was the residents themselves who came to the rescue and helped each other.

'There was also a Covid-19 floor – how do you evacuate that? Do you even care about Covid-19 at this point? No, you don't. I saw a big DHL truck so I stopped the driver and told him to take some of the injured. He told me he had dead bodies with him and couldn't leave them on the road.'

Rita paused and exhaled.

I couldn't help but notice how composed she was and in control of her narrative. I didn't expect her to be so calm and collected.

'I couldn't walk anymore. I had so much glass in my body. I was bleeding a lot.'

She showed me a photo of herself from that day, which she had sent to her parents. Her face looked swollen, with cuts and blood all over it, but, surprisingly, she was smiling.

'I had to,' she said, explaining the smile. 'I was helplessly proving to my parents that I was ok. But I was not.'

Today, Rita's physical injuries have healed, but she suffers from a lingering trauma and permanent hearing loss in one of her ears.

She moved to Marseilles in France in 2021, looking for a better and safer future. Thousands of doctors took a similar decision to emigrate, many of them after 4 August, impelled by the country's economic crisis and the calamitous explosion.

Rita and I chat every now and then over social media.

'I am so grateful I got the chance to leave. Leaving was the best thing to do for my mental health. I can say with absolute confidence that 4 August has scarred us all forever. Maybe those who died that day are not suffering anymore the way we are. They killed a whole city. My spirit is dead. I was proud of myself as I was one of the few female cardiologists in training in Lebanon. I was working hard, I was ambitious, now I don't care. This country steals your innocence, your safety, your ambition. You have no value as a human being.'

LAURE AL ALAM

'They sent them to their death.'

A few kilometres from Saint George Hospital, Laure, a young nurse working with the Beirut firefighters brigade, was having coffee with her colleague and best friend Sahar before they were called to the Beirut port on 4 August to extinguish the fire.

'Close to 6:00 p.m., a fire alarm rang and we had to dispatch. It was just a normal call.'

The fire at the port had been on for at least 20 minutes before it was reported.

'It was my turn to go but Sahar told me to go home. We switched shifts and she went with the team to the port.'

Sahar was the only woman among the ten firefighters who went to the port that day.

'She was being a good friend. She lived nearby, whereas I lived three hours away from Beirut. I commute to work every day because rent is expensive here.'

Laure's monthly salary was just 58 USD, when I interviewed her in 2021. It had lost 95 per cent of its value since 2019. She could not afford a home in Beirut.

'I was getting ready to go back to my house in the north when we were told there was a fire at the port. Someone said it was fireworks but we had no idea what it really was. If my colleagues knew what was in there, they might not have gone. They left just like they would have for any other mission and that unit specifically was very driven, passionate and reckless.'

Laure paused briefly, as if hesitating to say what came next.

'In reality, they sent them to their death. No one told them what was in that burning warehouse, no one.'

The official Lebanese narrative claims that the fire that afternoon was the result of welding work carried out at the warehouse earlier in the day. But that narrative has been seriously challenged by an investigation by Forensic Architecture in 2023 that proves, through fire simulations using videos and photos analysis from the explosion, that welding could not be the cause of the fire. The origin of the fire remains unknown to this day.

'They knew what was burning inside and they let it burn without warning anyone.'

Once at the port, and seeing the magnitude of the fire, the firefighters called for additional support, according to Laure. But right when another unit of firefighters were getting ready to leave, the explosion happened.

'The timing saved many, because if they had stayed in this building where we are, inside the rooms, or got to the port, many more would have died.

'I find it absurd that the timing of the blast saved many, but it is true. I am not talking about the firefighters only. It was the summer, people went home early from work or worked from home because of

Covid. Many people were staying in the mountains in August. I always replay the scenario in my head wondering what it would have looked like had this blast gone off in a different hour or different month or even different day. My mother was driving my daughter on the port road the day before at 6.07 p.m. I still get nauseous thinking about it.

'I don't remember much. I was outdoors, thank God. I remember how dusty it was. Everything turned grey after the blast. I collapsed and I was screaming and crying. I couldn't help anyone. There was no ambulance or department left. I don't like to recall the details. It drains me.'

The headquarters of the fire brigade, less than a kilometre away from the port, was completely destroyed on 4 August. Laure was miraculously unhurt.

When we met a year later, the firefighters' headquarters was still being rebuilt. The reconstruction was slow and dependent on money coming from donor organizations. Such was the case of most of the rebuilding in Beirut.

We sat in the newly renovated office of Lieutenant Ali Najm, head of public relations at the brigade. Laure was in her military uniform. She tried to smile but I could feel how uncomfortable she was talking to me. She could not wait to leave the interview, which all in all lasted just about 40 minutes.

She had to get clearance from the lieutenant to talk to me, maybe that's why she was so nervous, although he did not sit with us in the room. Or maybe it was just the guilt of surviving, the guilt of having switched shifts with her best friend.

'Everything here reminds me of them, reminds me of Sahar. You cannot forget. They live with us.'

She told me that she had not been in the room where she used to hang out with Sahar since the blast. The two were very close. Sahar, a passionate nurse and firefighter, as Laure described her, was engaged and about to get married in 2021. The two women confided in each other and spent most of their days together.

'I remember that afternoon she came and laid her head on my shoulder. She never did that before. Something was off. I asked her if she was okay, and she said yes and said we should lay down. We had a brief private discussion and then she slept a bit. When she woke up, I made coffee and that's when the fire alarm rang.'

Laure started tearing up. I couldn't easily connect with her emotionally or physically. There was a wide physical distance between us because of social distancing rules but it wasn't just that. She was not at ease sitting with me. I didn't know if it was because we were in her supervisor's office or because she was clearly still extremely traumatized. It put me under extreme pressure to carefully craft my questions and avoid pushing Laure. As a journalist, I had been trained in interviewing survivors' of violence but I always found it tricky to talk to those who had clearly not even begun to process their traumas. Laure was not getting any psychological help.

'I hate looking at the port. I can't look at it. I lost ten friends all at once, ten coffins all at once. I spent two weeks waiting for them, waiting for their bodies to be found. They told me to stop hoping for anyone to be alive because the area was completely erased. But I kept hoping until we found the last body.'

Laure was calm but I could feel she was getting angry.

'They [the politicians] knew about the ammonium nitrate, they knew about everything. This is not a work accident. They knew about the nitrate and they stayed silent. If my colleagues knew there was nitrate, they would not have gone down there. They would have at least helped evacuate people, take them to safety. I don't know, there were other useful things they could have done. I can't say more than that. I am not allowed to.'

Laure paused. She stood up and looked away.

'Why didn't I go with her? Why did Sahar go? Why not me? It's absurd. Why did she die and I stayed alive?'

She paused again and then looked at me. 'Are we done yet?'

I was not done but I felt guilty keeping her. I nodded. Without another word, she left.

Tragedy and Loss

SOUHA GEITANI

*'You go to a hospital to live, but my husband died
in a hospital, and there was nothing to save him.'*

Even before the current crisis, the Lebanese were struggling with the
lack of job opportunities and political instability. Many were forced
to emigrate in order to provide for their families. As a result, many
women found themselves alone with their kids, while their husbands
worked in Africa or the Gulf. Souha was one of those women.

Her husband Jihad had been working in Nigeria for many years.
She raised her daughter Gemma, who in 2022 was 9 years old, and
her son Karl, 12 years old, all alone.

'It always felt like I carried a burden until he was back home.
There were so many decisions I just could not make alone. It was
hard. I remember Karl would get sick and I would have to take
him all alone in the middle of the night to a hospital. This is the
price that women here pay for their husbands to make ends meet
because our politicians never did their job, to keep our men here.'

In the summer of 2020, Jihad finally came back to Lebanon to
visit his family. He had been absent for more than seven months
because of the Covid-19 pandemic and the flight disruptions across
the world.

But when he came home, it was not for a holiday.

Instead, on 4 August, Jihad was with his daughter at Saint George Hospital in Beirut. On her sixth birthday, Gemma had been diagnosed with Hodgkin lymphoma, a blood cancer. She had started treatment in Beirut more than a month before her father's arrival, and he was spending his time by her side at the hospital.

'That day he bought gifts for everyone: he got Gemma swimming goggles that she wanted and he gave me new pyjamas as I was sleeping at the hospital all the time. He even bought gifts for my parents. We had lunch together. While we were eating I told him that he smelled weird today, and asked what perfume he had on. He said he didn't have any. Then I asked him what he used in the shower. Gemma also told him he smelled weird. I think it was the smell of death.

'I don't know why but I was not feeling well at the hospital anymore. I was suffocating. When the doctor came for the rounds, I asked him if we could leave that day. He said we could leave the next morning. Jihad paid the bill.

'Then he said he was tired, so he took a nap. My brother called him at 5:30 p.m. and asked him to come play cards with him. Jihad told him he wasn't leaving the hospital, that he was sleeping there. He did not want to leave.'

Souha was tearing up but she continued.

'We were on the ninth floor so we could see how big the fire was. I was trembling and Jihad asked why I was so scared. He told me maybe it's a few men burning tyres.'

It was common that year for demonstrators to block roads with burning tyres in protest at the economic crisis and the incompetence of the government.

'I went to ask the nurses about the fire. As I walked back into the room, I saw the buildings in the distance exploding and I remembered saying "God help them", thinking it wouldn't get to us. And then, everything exploded. All I remember is that I stood up and was going to check on Gemma when I stumbled upon Jihad on the floor.

'There was no blood coming out of him at first, but his eyes were closed. I heard him breathe fast, so to me he was okay. I was trying to save Gemma first, because she was intubated and had an implanted port. A few minutes later, I saw Jihad bleeding from his ear and nose. I started screaming, but no one answered.

'I called my brother-in-law and told him I had no idea what was happening. The world seemed to have collapsed on us and I needed a car. I called my brother to find us another hospital. I couldn't get out of the room because of the rubble. I was screaming but no one was replying. An assistant nurse came to help me, her leg was injured. She helped me plug out the port and the tubes from Gemma. In the next room, a girl who had leukaemia and was injured, eventually died. Her mother gave me a piece of cloth and told me to put pressure on Jihad's head. But no one was coming to take him.

'I went nine floors down, barefoot on broken glass and rubble. I couldn't find any doctors to help me. I ended up calling a doctor and he told me to find the injury in his head and put pressure on the area. I turned his head to see where the injury was and his brains literally disintegrated in my hands.'

She paused and then sobbed. I started tearing up too. This was overwhelming. I met Souha, who is a distant cousin of mine, a few times throughout my work on the book. Sitting with her each time was excruciatingly painful for both of us.

'I walked down again, nine floors, barefoot and on broken glass, looking for a doctor, and I finally found someone. He came up with me and told me Jihad needed to be intubated, but he could not do anything. No one wanted to take him down. Everyone told me he was too heavy – a "heavy corpse" they kept repeating. I started removing the rubble with my bare hands and I found a wheelchair. I went back down the nine floors.

'I found some men and begged them to come up. I bribed them. The men carried him on the wheelchair. I was in front of them removing the rubble, clearing the way.

'Nine floors down, barefoot, once again.

'I saw a lot of injured people on the way down – people crying and people moaning, but I was blocking everything. I was focused on saving Jihad. It was only when we got out of the building that I realized the nightmare I was in.'

Saint George Hospital turned into one of the worst disaster zones in the city that evening. Twenty people died there, including four nurses.

'There were injured people everywhere, dead people left and right. I remember seeing people in hospital robes soaked in blood. People dead in cars. I started running around the street like a madwoman, trying to see which car was open or had keys so I could take him to another hospital. I could not remember where our car was. Then, my brother arrived on a motorbike. He stopped an old gold Dacia car. We put my husband in the back, but the man inside was screaming. He didn't want to have Jihad with him. He could tell he was dead. My brother went in the trunk of the car.'

Souha looked at her phone.

'My family was calling me and I could not pick up. I remember answering my dad, and I was about to tell him what happened but then I remembered he had high blood pressure. I told him "Akh Dad".'

'Akh' in Arabic is an expression used when someone is in pain.

'But then I said we were okay.'

Souha sobbed.

'You go to a hospital to live, but my husband died in a hospital, and there was nothing to save him. His head looked like a basketball, his eyes were so big, as big as a tennis ball. Each of them pitch-black.'

She was now weeping continuously. I felt uncomfortable and asked her to take a break.

'This is our last family photo together.'

She stood up and showed me a family photo she had on a table in her living room.

'Gemma was already losing her hair and I remember she had a bruise too. She fell down while playing on her bike. I photoshopped it so it wouldn't look like she had no hair and had a bruise. I didn't want her to remember that.'

Then she showed me photos and videos of 4 August on her phone. It included a video of the fire and I could hear Jihad in the background asking her if she was afraid. There was another one outside the hospital with him on the wheelchair. This one will haunt me forever. I asked her why she kept them.

'I don't look at them so often but I keep them so I can show people the amount of pain that I have been through. No one asked about us, no one. Imagine, the joke that this government is. First, they misspelled his name. Then someone highly ranked in the army called me to offer me condolences. He said he was sorry for the death of my son Gemma! I told him, first of all, Gemma is my daughter, and she didn't die. It's my husband who did. That's how clueless they are. He told me he was calling to invite me to a candlelight vigil at the port. I told him what is that going to bring me? Go get me justice, for once in history, show us that you are capable of holding criminals accountable.'

Souha's anger echoed that of many women in this book, searching in vain for accountability they may never obtain. The feeling of injustice is maddening and I feel it too. My paternal grandmother lost her husband too, at a young age, like Souha. My uncle and father were respectively four and five years old when it happened. The criminal who killed my grandfather barely served any time in prison. My grandmother conformed to the reality of that time. Maybe she knew that fighting for justice was hopeless.

'When your dad paid his condolences to me, he told me about his childhood and he even cried,' Souha tells me, referring to my father.

I started tearing up again.

'My coffee mug in the hospital room did not break, Gemma's spaghetti plate was untouched, but Jihad died. Why?'

Souha picked up her phone again and asked me if she could read a text she had written for Jihad's funeral. I nodded.

'You left me standing here, alone and broken. You always told me not to worry, you told me that everything passes, nothing lasts forever. But, my pain will last forever. I blame myself every day. I once told our children that death only comes to take the elderly, and now they ask me why it took you away and I have no answer. I don't know what to tell them without breaking them. I told them you were kind and we were becoming too many on this planet. God needs angels with him, angels to protect us, and he cannot take the bad guys so he chose you.'

Then, almost as if whispering, she told me: 'Yesterday was our wedding anniversary – 12 years. We promised each other to be together forever. Till death do us apart. And it did. But it's not death that took him away, it's the criminals in power who took him away from me.'

One day, Souha posted a video on Instagram of a little bird chasing Gemma and clinging to her shoulder, pausing on her palm. The bird would not leave her. I saw the video and reacted. It was beautiful, after all, birds don't usually stick to people like that.

'It's a message from heaven,' responded Souha, 'that he is still with us.'

MELANIE DAGHER

'I've lost my fingers. Can you help me pick up my fingers?'

Melanie embodies in many ways the Lebanese identity crisis that many of us grapple with. That feeling of being continually torn between wanting to stay in Lebanon and wanting to leave. The conflicted feelings of feeling at home but also not exactly identifying with and assimilating to everything in it. Loving Lebanon while also hating it. Eagerly wanting to leave it but then once out, longing for it. It's as if we are never whole or complete in one place. We scatter bits and pieces of ourselves here and there, hoping to find that stillness that evokes home.

'I was living in Lebanon by mistake,' she told me. 'There was a revolution here,' referring to the October 2019 uprising. Mass protests were sparked by the decision of the government to increase taxes, including on WhatsApp calls, in an attempt to increase its dwindling revenues. Roads were blocked almost every day and a lot of businesses, institutions, and even embassies shut down. 'So, they stopped working at the German Embassy and they lost my file.'

Melanie had applied to renew her visa to return to Berlin where she had been living before 2019.

'And then when I applied again, in 2020, it was a time when Germany was doing an investigation on Hezbollah to officially state them as a terrorist group. Germany designated Hezbollah as a terrorist organization in April 2020.

'And during that time, they were not issuing visas to Lebanese people, out of security. So, yeah, I was stuck here, I was not supposed to be in Lebanon. I was supposed to go back to my job.'

Four days before 4 August, Melanie had moved to a new flat in Beirut's Mar Mikhael neighbourhood. It's a historic district with beautiful traditional Lebanese houses, known for its bustling streets, lively bars, and excellent restaurants.

'My new apartment was in front of that gas station that is still destroyed. The port is directly in front and there was nothing between us. Everything was new and I had just moved my furniture and all my belongings.

'The worst part is, that day, I was finally feeling happy about living in Lebanon. I often grappled with my feelings towards Lebanon. I even told my dad that day that I did not want to go back to Europe anymore. I was actually happy here. It was hard for me in Europe to define who I was. In Lebanon, I felt like I was someone.

'My father was proud of me and told me he knew this day would come, where I would believe in my country.

'He was exaggerating. It was not really that. I loved Lebanon but I still struggled to fit in. Our parents lived through the civil war and what came after, but they are kind of in denial. I am not sure why they are such believers in this country. Anyway, my dad basically gave me a glorifying speech about Lebanon that made no sense a few hours later.'

Around 6:00 p.m., Melanie was at home with a friend having dinner. What comes next is her detailed account, as she narrated it in English, relentlessly, without even taking a breath.

'I was so close to the explosion that I didn't hear it.

'You know, the pressure was so big that I didn't even feel like it was an explosion. I remember that I heard the sound of low planes flying above my head and then everything turned black. I flew.

'I went from standing in my living room to being on the floor in my bedroom. I flew across my home and I don't know what hit me. I know that I was injured, but I don't know how it happened.

'My first reflex was to think of my friend. Her name is Lynn. She wasn't conscious because the wall that was between me and my neighbour fell on us. I received the door, I think, on my neck.

'In my head, the explosion happened in my building. The ceiling was open so we could see the sky. I carried her, and to carry her I had to walk over a lot of broken glass. It cut my leg open, but I had no choice.

'I remember that I saw my neighbour's shoes in my flat. I was going down the stairs and I heard someone screaming on the first floor. It was an old woman, alone, covered in blood, and her flat was even more destroyed than mine. She told me, "Please, I've lost my fingers. Can you help me pick up my fingers?" I just didn't think anymore.

'I started picking up fingers from the floor and I was holding them. I was holding her and my friend and I had no clue what was going on.

'I had no clue who was alive, who was not. In my head, it was war.

'I carried both of them. Two women. The old woman, I think she was from Syria. She was just repeatedly screaming. I still had the fingers in my hand. The entrance door was blocked by a lot of rubble, things that flew over, like tables and chairs. I got out and I left my friend on the floor where there were no windows, thinking probably she would be safe as she couldn't walk. I thought more airstrikes were coming.

'I climbed up on top of the rubble with the old woman and that is where I saw Mar Mikhael, an apocalyptic scene out of a bad movie.

'The first thing I saw was a gas station and a worker whose body was completely dismantled. His leg was somewhere, and his arm somewhere else. He passed away obviously on the ground.

'I turned and I saw a guy who was our doorman, who was on the floor and his face was gone. I couldn't distinguish his nose, from his eyes, from his mouth. He was bleeding a lot. And then he was just crying and asking me to help him. He was saying that he was dying. He was just repeating that he's going to die.

'Between him, the scene that I saw and the fingers in my hands, everything started to become very blurry. And I felt like my fingers were numb. I think I was just losing too much blood. I couldn't walk anymore.

'And then it all resumed again, like a movie, with the sound of this old woman screaming in my ears. And this is where I realized that no one's looking at us. I'm the only semi-functioning person among people dying. I had to do something. I couldn't just give up.

'I went down to the street, and took the old woman with me. The cars were not stopping. I stopped a Red Cross ambulance. I saw maybe 100 people on top of each other. It was all red. I could only see blood. I begged the driver to take her. I put her in the van, gave him the fingers, and went back to take care of the doorman.

'Now, I realize that carrying those fingers was probably useless, as we had no ice. I just started carrying the doorman, not knowing what I was doing.

'I was carrying him. I fell as he was too heavy to carry. In my head, I was killing him. No one looked at me. Everyone around me was even worse. I didn't know what to do anymore. At some point I remember I sat on the floor with him and I felt that he was passing away. You really feel it. You feel the body change. It becomes heavier. And then a guy comes and says he is a doctor and that I should stop looking at the man as he was dead.

'I had watched him for the past fifteen minutes. I was holding onto him like I was holding onto my life.

'I don't know why. I felt like if I let him go, he would die, although he was already dead.'

Melanie finally paused.

I breathed. I thought I had been holding my breath all along. It felt like I was there, experiencing this all with her once again – the darkest moments of her life.

'It's hard to talk about it.' She started tearing up, although I did not expect her to. She was just like Rita, so placid. 'I saw a pregnant woman beheaded, a guy without eyes, I saw every single thing.'

Melanie said she fainted at some point and was taken to a hospital. She did not remember the ride.

Her friend made it out alive, but Melanie didn't discover the fate of the old woman.

She picked up the story from when she was at the hospital, on a wheelchair attached to an IV, desperately waiting for someone to stitch up her head.

'An ambulance arrived. And the nurse that was inside went down and ran towards me. I thought, finally, someone was going to help me. But she actually told me she had to take my chair. She put me on the floor. The hospital was running out of everything.

'I thought I was dying. I was on the floor and the blood circled around me getting bigger and bigger. I was just watching myself die.

'And that's when my dad arrived and went crazy. He carried me. They took me to the emergency room and they started stitching me without any anaesthesia and with a mobile phone flashlight, because there was no power. It was the most painful thing ever.'

Many hospitals that night operated on the injured without the use of electricity. Lebanon was covered in darkness even before the blast. Power cuts had always been a recurrent problem since the end of the civil war, but they just became more frequent that summer with the economic crisis and the fuel shortages. Outages lasted for up to 23 hours in some regions.

The headquarters of the archaic state-owned electricity company, EDL, whose expenses equate to half of Lebanon's public debt, were completely destroyed on 4 August. The blast put the last nail in its coffin.

A few weeks after recovering from her wounds, Melanie started volunteering in Beirut at what was known as Base Camp, a citizens-led initiative providing help and relief to those affected by the explosion and the economic crisis. It was an impressive operation. People from across the country and the world came together to help in the absence of any governmental response.

'I work in fashion, I couldn't see myself going back to that. It didn't make sense. And I couldn't see myself staying home, doing nothing or overthinking. I felt comfortable being around people that were more injured than me or that were suffering more than me, not because I wanted them to, but because I felt like I belonged with them. That is why I couldn't leave the country. Everyone was like, leave. What are you still doing here?

'And now it's been a year and I might leave at the end of the month. I don't know yet, depending on the visa. But it was impossible for me to leave before. I couldn't see myself going somewhere where no one understands what I had been through. It is like Stockholm syndrome or a toxic relationship where your husband is beating you and you cannot leave. That's what Lebanon feels to me. It is not easy to leave.'

When I last checked in with Melanie, she had left Lebanon and was living in Paris.

3

Mayhem

*'It was chaos. There were no hospitals left and
the roads were blocked.'*

Nour is my youngest sister's best friend. I have known her since she
was a child.

She had just turned 25 in the summer of 2020 and was dedicating
all her energy and time to the Lebanese Red Cross, volunteering as
an emergency medical technician.

The LRC is the main provider of ambulances and blood
transfusion across the country. It provides free medical services to
hundreds of thousands of people every year, operating dozens of
primary healthcare centres, and nine mobile clinics. It has been
instrumental in responding to the shortage of medicine and access
to healthcare amid Lebanon's economic crisis.

Nour was not on duty on 4 August.

'I was home, on my computer, and I remember I felt a pressure.
Then I saw dust everywhere and everything was flying. I ducked
under the table.'

She was not hurt and luckily her apartment remained intact.
Nour lived in Badaro, a largely residential neighbourhood in Beirut,

located about 6 kilometres from the epicentre of the blast. Her first reaction was to rush to her sister who lived in the same building.

'My sister's house was full of glass, but she was so calm. She even started cleaning.'

Nour's sister is about 20 years older than her and is a survivor of the Lebanese civil war.

'I never lived through the war. I felt clueless. She, on the hand, seemed to understand what was going on.

'Then I saw the messages flooding in on the Red Cross WhatsApp group. What should we do? Should we go to the Red Cross centre? We usually get our instructions from the team leader but she said, "Stay at home, we don't know what's going on", and her phone switched off, she disappeared.'

Nour was still trying to make sense of what happened when she got a desperate call from a friend of hers crying for help.

'My friend was screaming: "Nour, my dad is in Gemmayzeh, we can't reach out to him and the Red Cross is not responding."'

Nour called the Red Cross centre as well as their hotline but no one picked up.

'This was 10 minutes after the explosion. I called a colleague who was on duty, she was in shock and seemed clueless.

'My friend called me again, screaming and crying: "Please help me, we can't find my father. Nour please help me. Why isn't the Red Cross answering?"'

That was when Nour realized something big had happened.

'I went down to my car. I had a Red Cross kit inside. I started driving. The roads were blocked. My friend called again, this time, she was with her father. We put on the video and I told her what to do. I remember how her father was laying down on the floor. His house was destroyed. Everyone around him was screaming and I was doing first aid on a video call. I told her to take him to the closest hospital. I was telling her how to carry him, how to lift him up. I was explaining everything in detail. At some point she screamed: "Dad! Dad . . . he stopped breathing!" And she hung up. My heart skipped a beat. I felt helpless. I wanted to get to her. I wanted to help her but I could not. Her father lived in Saudi Arabia and was visiting Lebanon that summer because his daughter gave birth.'

Nour kept driving and now was seeing lots of people walking injured on the streets.

'I saw a woman laying down on the floor. I had to stop and help. She was bleeding and there were two people standing next to her. I gave them something from my toolkit and asked them to put pressure on her wounds and then take her to the hospital. I was trying to park my car when I then saw one of our ambulances. It was empty, with the lights on. That was not right, I thought. I parked my car and started to run. I was running, holding my uniform and kit, and hearing people shouting: Red Cross! Red Cross! They asked me to come into the buildings. People were trapped inside. But as Red Cross volunteers we cannot do that. Our safety comes first. I kept saying I will come back. I was running and running. I passed our centre without realizing it. That is because not much was left of it.'

The Lebanese Red Cross centre in Beirut was completely destroyed on 4 August. Despite losing its vital headquarters that evening, the LRC still played a major role in helping the wounded across the city.

'I wore my uniform and went back on the streets. We started like a hospital tent for victims in the parking lot of the headquarters. Everything was chaotic, there was no lights, no electricity. We used flashlights and projectors to see. I helped sort the injured and it felt like an endless nightmare. So many people were running towards us, screaming and asking for help, and we did not have the capacity to help them all. It was so hard telling someone "I'm sorry, I can't do anything for you or your family member."'

Nour's voice began to break.

'I started to colour-code people. Green: you are good you can walk to the hospital. Yellow: we have to take you to the hospital.

Black: we can't do anything, they are dead. We were colour-coding people and the ambulances were coming to take them. We were trying to be as organized as possible, but people were screaming at us. They had to wait, sometimes for hours. We tried to calm people down. We were trying to be emotionally there for them but we also had to switch off our own feelings. We had to stay strong. We get trained for a mass-casualty incident. But this was different. It was chaos. There were no hospitals left and the roads were blocked. We were trying to find a way for the ambulances to move. We had to help, we had to come up with solutions, and no one else was helping. We did not see the police or anyone from the army helping. Not one politician showed up. It was citizens who were removing the rubble, cleaning. People were just helping each other, no one else was there.'

I asked Nour what happened to her friend's dad.

'He eventually died. I wanted to go check up on him but the team leader told me I can't prioritize. I have to help other people. The first time I actually spoke to my friend was a month ago, that's almost a year later. I couldn't find the words before. I apologized for not helping her. I am sorry I could not do anything.'

Nour started crying. She seemed broken and fragile.

Her father was very sick and passed away before the explosion. It was a traumatic experience for her. Then came the blast. It took her many months to start processing all the distress, to allow the pain to sink in, to cry. She did not seek any counselling, thinking she was not ready to open up.

'I wanted things to go at my own pace, but yes, I was traumatized. This is my first time recalling in detail the explosion. When I moved to London after the blast, there was an underground next to us and the house shakes a bit every time a train goes by. The first time it happened I covered myself, I went under the table. I was clearly not well.'

Nour showed me a tattoo on her triceps that she got following 4 August. It was an hourglass.

'Time is priceless and volatile. It takes only a few seconds for you to lose everything in your life.'

KARINE MATTAR

'The doctors were like zombies, there was blood everywhere, they didn't know what to do.'

'I thought an airplane crashed down on the building next to us. But I didn't really care about what happened. I just wanted to save my eyes. I didn't notice my other injuries. The first thing I realized was that I couldn't see. I told my partner: "My eyes, please my eyes."'

Karine was home when the blast rocked Beirut on 4 August. Her apartment was in Achrafieh, an upscale neighbourhood in the east of the city, and one of the worst-hit areas. The windows of her balcony collapsed on her small body, severely injuring one of her eyes and her hand.

'It's my right hand, I can't open it and close it,' she told me as she helplessly tried to wiggle her fingers.

'The flesh was coming out of my hand. But I felt nothing at that time. I actually think my hand saved my eyes. It protected my eyes.'

A few minutes after the blast, Karine left the apartment with her boyfriend, who was not injured, looking for the nearest hospital in the city. She did not know she was actually embarking on the longest journey of her life.

'We went to the first hospital, they told me that they could not take me in. We were there early but the hospital was damaged and they were clueless. They sent us away. We went to another hospital, it was relatively calm. This time they put me on a wheelchair, cleaned my wounds, and I waited. But two minutes later, the hospital was flooded with people. It was a tsunami. Unbelievable. A nightmare. Injured people everywhere. Their situation was worse than mine. Zein [her partner] tried to block my view so I don't see what was around me, but it was inevitable. Beside me was a little boy, his hand was cut off. In front of me was a guy with an open skull. All the doctors were trying to help him. There was also this guy with pierced lungs. He was coughing blood and then lost consciousness. I wasn't a priority anymore. They didn't close my wounds. I understood later on that I needed surgery and they could not do it. They even took my wheelchair. I ended up sitting on the street.'

More than 6,000 people were injured that evening, overwhelming the country's hospitals. Thousands flocked to medical centres in and outside Beirut. Many hospitals turned them down either because they were destroyed or overcrowded. Many medical centres also had no supplies left to treat the injured. Hospitals were already struggling with a shortage of supplies because of the economic crisis, and many treated the injured with the bare minimum of care. People had to drive to the far north and far south to find help. Karine's family debated whether to drive her to a hospital in the mountains. She could have been experiencing internal head bleeding.

'They took the risk and drove me to another hospital, outside of Beirut, in the mountains where my parents usually spend their summers. This time it was far. The car ride was really long. The roads were blocked. Rubble. Cars. Traffic jam. Longest ride of my life. Once arrived, I thought the hospital would be empty since it is far. But it wasn't. It was worse. The doctors were like zombies, there was blood everywhere, they didn't know what to do. I remember we were in the parking lot. I started to have an anxiety attack. I took off my bra. I could not breathe.'

Karine's voice broke here.

'I could not see the end of this nightmare. I thought I was going to die. We were jumping from one hospital to another and no one was helping. That's when my brother-in-law literally kidnapped a doctor. The doctor checked me, said he could not help, and sent me to a clinic in another town to see an eye doctor. It was a 10-minute drive but also felt like forever. I get there. There were two injured persons ahead of me. I had to wait, yet again. Then the doctor saw me and told me I needed surgery but said he could not do it. I had to find a hospital.'

Karine decided to return to the last hospital she had visited. Her eye needed urgent attention, she could not wait. She called a friend who worked in the medical field, begging her to find a surgeon who would operate on her that evening.

'This time, I entered a patient's room. I saw a nun. I said I need a bed for my operation. She told me if you find anything, a bed, a chair, a couch, sit on it. Imagine, I started running around, despite my injuries, looking for something. We divided the hospital floors between us, my sister, her husband, my boyfriend and me. Each one was looking on one floor. We finally found a bed. It was 3 a.m.'

Karine's only choice by then was to be operated on by a general practitioner, as no specialists were available.

'I entered the operating room. Another person was there under surgery. The doctors were shocked when they saw me. I did not even have any IV serum, I was not prepped for a surgery, nothing. I sat down on a chair. No beds available. The doctor was operating on my eye. He was gentle, but I was awake as they didn't have time to do a general anaesthesia. I was awake and I could hear everything. I heard the doctor asking for things, give me this and that. Noting was available. I kept hearing someone saying "we don't have, we don't have . . ." At some point the doctor said: "I can't see anything." The nurse answered: "The power has been cut." She used her phone's light to help the doctor operate. Another doctor came to operate on my hand at the same time.'

A year later, when we met, Karine's eye was back to normal but not her hand. The operation that night had not been successful. She was still getting physical therapy but her hand was not fully functional. Another operation was not going to work and was too risky, she tells me.

Karine owns a well-known nursery in Beirut and though the blast only slightly damaged her business, it affected her ability to work.

'I used to do everything. In the morning when we receive the children, I take their bags, I carry them, but now I ask for help. I can't hold the children anymore. It makes me sad. There is mother, a client of mine, who told a friend that I lost the spark in my eyes, I had a spark in my eyes and I lost it. Now I would do everything to have it back.'

4

Stamina

PAMELA ZEINOUN

*'I kept pinching them. I wanted them to cry to
make sure they were alive.'*

Pamela always knew she wanted to be in medicine. Her love of
babies meant paediatrics was a natural choice. She wanted hands-on
experience and loved the human connection that comes with being
a nurse. She specialized in newborn intensive care even though
here she would often be exposed to suffering and death among tiny
human beings who had just seen the light of the day.

'The first baby I saw die was a traumatizing experience. He had
been in the ICU for more than a year. He had become our baby.
We played with him. We loved him. Out of the blue, we were told
he died. He had respiratory problems. It was very tough.'

On the afternoon of 4 August the 27-year-old paediatric nurse
was working at the Newborn Intensive Care Unit of Saint George
Hospital. She was doing her usual rounds, checking on babies and
briefing their families.

'I was in the premature babies' section with two of my
colleagues, a few minutes before 6 p.m. We were assisting a family,
they were visiting their baby. I was talking to them. Then I left for
the neo-natal section where I had a patient. And I decided to call

my mother, I always call her at that time of the day. As we were speaking, I heard a first loud boom, it was strong, I could tell it was not normal. I remember turning around to the window and telling my mother that I heard an explosion. My mother was outside of Beirut, very far from the port, but she told me she heard it too. A couple of seconds later, I felt the floor jumping beneath me. My reaction was to move away from the window, the phone was still in my hand. There was a big closet, the drawers knocked me down. It fell on me and threw me on the floor. Everything collapsed on my head. The ceiling, the glass, the steel.'

The first thought that came to Pamela's mind was the safety of the babies.

'I could not get to the premature baby from where I was. There was a collapsed ceiling between me and the incubator. I could see the baby, she was fine but I could not remove the rubble. I decided to leave and go to where I was before the explosion.'

Pamela told me that the next part was still a bit blurry in her mind. I insisted she should try to remember as much as she could. Despite her traumatic experience she seemed in control of her narrative, and she actually ended up remembering many details about the heroic work she did that day.

'There was no power. It was a long corridor. I remember shouting the name of one of our colleagues who was pregnant. I tripped over two nurses. They were both soaked in blood. They had cuts in their heads. They were holding hands. The pregnant one, that's the colleague I was shouting for, had her hand on her belly. I tried to speak to them but they looked at me and had a blank stare. They weren't screaming or crying but they were not responsive. I had injuries but I looked okay. I worried they weren't going to make it. I later found out that they could not hear me and they couldn't see because there was blood in their eyes. They both don't remember seeing me up to this day.

'I left them, I made sure the pregnant one was not bleeding from her vagina. The hardest part was the smell, there was a lot of dust, you couldn't breathe. It was really tough.

'I tried to save the four babies in the premature recovery department, as I could not get to the NICU baby. I remember carrying one of the babies and giving it to her mother. I told her to leave immediately for another hospital. I had no idea what was outside, that most of Beirut's hospitals were gone. All of the incubators had moved and were damaged but the babies were still sleeping in them. I started removing the babies one after the other. I kept telling myself I just hope they are not injured because I would not be able to do anything.

'I saw them sleeping but I did not know if they were dead or alive. The incubators, though damaged, somehow protected them.

'I carried the three premature babies in my arms.

'My constant worry was their body temperature, I kept thinking they would get cold.

'The dad of the baby I sent away was still there. I tried to talk to him, told him to help me fetch pyjamas for the babies from a drawer, because they were in diapers. But I couldn't speak, I couldn't utter a word. I gestured with my hands. He understood. He opened the drawer and gave me the pyjamas. I don't know why I couldn't talk. It's as if I was trying to channel all of my power into saving these babies, as though, if I uttered a word I would lose that power, I would lose control. I was fully focused on the babies.

'He gave me things I put on top of the babies, but by the time I was out of the hospital, everything fell down, they were naked in my arms.

'I remember walking down the exit stairs and the ramp was full of blood. I would put out my hand and feel like I am slipping. There was also blood on the floor. There was rubble. There were nurses trying to take patients on pieces of fallen ceiling because there were no beds or stretchers. I was going down and the mother with the baby was in front, the father behind, and me in the middle. The mother would slip, I would help her, I would slip, the father would help me. That's how we went four floors down. I walked slowly, in between the rubble, holding them tight in my arms. I did not know if they were dead or alive.'

Pamela got out of the hospital building, the three premature babies still in her arms, and sat down inside the entrance booth of the hospital to decide what to do next. At that moment a photojournalist took a photo of her. It went viral.

'I needed to know what was happening to know what to do next. I was getting scared. People were telling me to leave because there would be another air strike. People thought there was an air strike. I wanted to make sure the babies were alive. I stimulated them manually a bit, they moved. I had no monitor, nothing. I made sure they were fine.

'I started asking people to give me their clothes. I would wrap each kid with whatever I had. A doctor came to me and wanted to help. I refused to give the babies to him or to anyone. I felt responsible for all three. Two of them were twins. But he told me to follow him to the emergency. When we got there, I started crying, I realized that I was not going to be able to get help for those babies. I was also wondering about the girl I left in the NICU, wondering if someone was finally able to save her.'

Pamela said that was when she and the doctor decided to leave the hospital. They walked towards another nearby clinic, thinking like many survivors in this book, that they would get help there.

'They told me I could not get in, there were no incubators anymore, all were damaged. That is when I started realizing how huge this was, that it went beyond our hospital, beyond that street. I stopped at another hospital, the same, this time the security in charge of the hospital gave me his vest to apologize for not being able to let me into the hospital. He told me to wrap the babies with it. It was August but they were tiny. Their temperature had to stay at 35 degrees. They were getting heat from my body, skin to skin, and I wrapped them in the vest.

'I started running with the babies in my arms, I had no time to lose. On my way I heard people screaming next to me "Oh God! Oh God!" It scared me even more. I didn't know if I was doing the right thing.

'At some point I slipped and fell but the babies stayed in my arms. I tried to go behind someone on a bike, I couldn't. I hitched a ride but there was too much traffic, so I got out and started walking again.

'I was on the highway. That's when a baby slipped and I managed to grab him by his feet, just before he hit ground. It was terrifying.

'I kept pinching them. I wanted them to cry to make sure they were alive. I walked with them for an hour and a half on the highway. I thought we would never make it. I wanted to give up many times, but the doctor and I encouraged each other.'

They eventually managed to get a ride from a passing car.

I was getting really tired just listening to her account. It felt like an endless journey.

'I remember sitting in the middle. There was a driver, his daughter, his wife and their seven-year-old grandson. The boy looked at us petrified. I started crying. I felt so vulnerable. The doctor cried too. My arms were trembling. The woman was trying to soothe me. And just as we were arriving to the hospital one of the babies had an apnoea. He turned black, I thought he died. I gave the two others to the doctor and started stimulating him, his back, his legs, just so he cries. He wasn't responding. At the end, miraculously, he cried. He came back to life.'

Pamela and the doctor finally made it to a hospital outside Beirut and started frantically looking for incubators.

'No one would help me. I ended up finding one. I put all three babies in it. They were all alive.'

Her heroism that day is something to praise and admire. But the strength and composure of the young woman eventually gave way to what was only human, namely vulnerability and distress. For days, she told me, she couldn't eat. She lost 15 pounds. Though she claimed not to have PTSD, Pamela said she would jump at the slightest sound.

'August 5 I was back to work. Back on that floor. I was asked to come. There were tons of media requests. I went, looked around.

It was very calm but I was having flashbacks. I saw the incubators. The blood.'

Pamela says she didn't get any immediate leave to take time off work. It was only in December, four months later, that she got three weeks off, and they were unpaid.

I called her a year after our interview. She was still living with her parents and wanted to stay in Lebanon to 'fight'.

'I want to know who is responsible for that blast, who is responsible for me having to carry three premature babies and run for their lives. Someone is.'

Pamela has been in touch with the families of the babies she saved and often visits them. One of the infants is now living in France.

'I didn't just save them. They actually saved me too. I was so focused on them, their weight in my arms was a constant reminder that I had to go on, that I had no option, that I could not give up.'

STEPHANIE YAACOUB

'So many were taking their last breath while I helped two babies come to life that day.'

Stephanie is an Australian with Lebanese parents. She has spent her life moving back and forth between Lebanon and Australia. She was the chief Ob-gyn resident at Saint George Hospital on 4 August.

I know I keep going back to that hospital but it's for a good reason. It just so happens that some of the most powerful stories originated from that hospital, which had become a site of unremitting tragedy. Once a safe haven for the sick and the wounded, Saint George Hospital now resembled Dante's inferno.

Two years on, the hospital still felt like it was trapped in that inferno. Windows had still not been replaced, but were rather masked by wooden panels, blocking natural light from entering the rooms. Lifts were still not functioning properly. In some wards, including the maternity ward where Stephanie worked, time felt like it had stopped on 4 August.

In many ways, Saint George Hospital was a reflection of Beirut, a broken city now struggling to come back to life. Two years on, it was still not completely rebuilt.

Stephanie had three patients on the afternoon of 4 August 2020. One of them, Rita, was recovering from delivery and two others, Emmanuelle and Christelle, were about to give birth.

'We went to Emmanuelle's room and we were just joking with her and her husband that they were going to name their baby George at Saint George Hospital. I decided to help her push, cheering her on. We pushed her into the delivery room and then that's the famous video that her husband was recording.'

A video of Emmanuelle in the delivery room during the blast went viral on social media.

'I felt, first of all, what was an earthquake. My colleague Marianne, who was standing next to the window, said it's maybe a helicopter landing on the hospital's helipad, but she didn't even have time to finish her sentence before we heard a very loud bang. I found myself flung against the wall with Emmanuelle's bed pushed against me. The aluminium hit my head. I pushed the bed off me and I stood up.'

I expected Stephanie to tell me what happened next, but she shared something else.

'My heart just sank. You come to love Lebanon so much and you talk to all your friends who are Australian about this country. You tell them it is so beautiful. It's just got a bad reputation. But in reality, this is unfortunately Lebanon. We put on a facade that this country is magnificent and glorious, and you can come here and have an amazing time. Ski and go to the beach in the same day, but it's not.'

Stephanie, just like Melanie, wrestled with her conflicted feelings for Lebanon. Her family first came to Beirut when she was seven.

They left five years later because of instability in the country. At 18, she had returned and settled in Beirut to study medicine.

'I didn't like Lebanon first. I didn't think anything of it. But it just grew on me, I think. You never really feel like you belong, like you do in Lebanon. You just find your roots.'

I identify with these women. It is especially after you have lived abroad that the conflicted feelings surface. You have now tasted something different, drastically different. You like that difference but you don't love it yet. You are at peace abroad but it does not feel like home. Once back in Lebanon, you struggle with a lot of madness and chaos. You love it but you also hate it. It is a complicated relationship.

Back in the delivery room, Stephanie had to think quick. There was no time to lose. The baby was about to be born at any minute.

'I just went with my instinct, which was that I needed to hear that this baby was okay. I was jumping over rubble and pieces of I don't know what. And I kept saying, give me a fetal heartbeat, give me a fetal heartbeat. I was doing it anyways on my own. And then I heard the baby and the heartbeat was perfectly fine. I remember we all took a deep breath for a second. Emmanuelle was on the bed. She had calmed down when we told her that the baby was fine and she stayed surprisingly calm the whole time. Everything really does happen for a reason, because if George had been born just before the blast or when the blast happened, he would have been harmed.'

Her husband, Eddie, was very emotional because he was running to the waiting area to check on his mother. She had pneumothorax and broken ribs. He did an amazing job. He helped us move so much of the ceiling that had fallen onto the ground throughout the corridors because we were pretty much trapped in the delivery area.

There is a little pathway that goes between delivery rooms and there's no glass there. So, we thought that would be the safest place. Her husband and some midwives and myself moved her there. Unfortunately, she was in position to deliver her baby and her legs were up and facing the emergency exit. We kept trying to stand in front of that area throwing Betadine to keep her vagina as sterile as possible. But at that moment, they turned off the electricity. It was quite dark because there are no windows. Her doctor wasn't there yet. We would get the Doppler machine, which is like a small, hand-held, very old-school way of listening to the baby's heartbeat that runs on batteries. And it was halfway full of battery. And we didn't know how long it was going to take or how long the batteries would last. So very intermittently we would try and grab the baby's heartbeat.'

As Stephanie was trying to ensure a safe delivery for Emmanuelle, people around her were dying.

'One of the residents came to me and he said, "The patient in 512, he's not doing well at all. He has a head injury and is bleeding heavily."'

That was the husband of a patient of Stephanie's who had given birth the day before.

'He wasn't doing too well and they were carrying him down the stairs on a piece of ceiling. He had a severe intracranial bleeding and he didn't make it. Their baby was a day old.'

Stephanie was also called to check on a fellow nurse who was unconscious.

'It seemed like she had been long gone. Probably at the moment the explosion happened. I couldn't find any bleeding. I couldn't find anything to explain why that happened. But I kept looking for a pulse and I couldn't feel it. And I mean, it's so easy to say there's no pulse. You know, we have to move on. But I couldn't bring myself to make that decision. I kept trying to feel a pulse. There was no chest rise. She wasn't breathing or anything. But I screamed to someone to grab me a stethoscope to listen. Maybe I could hear a heartbeat. And then I told them to get the defibrillator just in case. We put the electrodes on, but there was nothing. I was doing CPR just to try. And the most surprising thing is that . . .'

Stephanie held her breath. We were sitting in my living room. She was the only interviewee to have visited me in my house.

'While I was doing chest compressions, her phone started ringing. Her family was calling to check on her.'

Stephanie paused. She cried. By now, it had become common for every woman I'd interviewed to break down. I was starting to get used to this. But I wasn't sure I was better at managing my feelings. It still felt uncomfortable.

'I think the worst part is that so many lives were lost that shouldn't have been lost in a hospital. That was the hardest thing for me. I know that people come to the hospital to be treated and to feel safe. And if that doesn't exist, then what does?'

At 6:08 p.m., Emmanuelle was ready to deliver. But the shock of the explosion prevented her from pushing. The baby's head moved up again. The mother was in distress.

'If the mom panics, then you've lost everything. I started looking into her eyes telling her we're all here. No one's going to leave you. It was getting dark. There was no power. My colleague held two phones to give us light, and we eventually had to use forceps. I just wanted to get the head out. Once his head was out, the rest of his body was easy to deliver. The birth of George, the exact moment that he cried, we all just paused. It was a miracle. That cry was probably the best thing I've ever heard in my life.'

Stephanie's relief was momentous. As soon as she was done with Emmanuelle and made sure she got out of the hospital with her baby safely, she had another patient to deliver.

'The parking lot across from the emergency room had been transformed into an ER. So Christelle was on a normal bed, sitting there in the parking lot. And I remember she looked at me and she's like, I'm not going to have my baby in a parking lot. The paediatric surgeon tried to see if we can get an ambulance. And I remember telling him, keep the ambulances for people that really need it. She's just in labour. He found an SUV that can take her. But can she sit? Probably not, because she has an epidural. She won't really be able to move around much. We had to sleep in the back seat of the Jeep. I carried her with the resident into the back seat of the car and her doctor was next to me. I went in the boot of the trunk of the car. I was putting my head under the headdress to make sure that she was okay. And I held her hand telling her, don't look outside, just keep looking at me. Everything's going to be okay. I asked the driver for his name. Turns out it was a paediatric resident who had had pelvic fractures. Imagine he had to drive us. I just kept begging him to please drive safe. There was so much traffic. We made it to a hospital outside of Beirut. People there were just screaming, saying you have to take us in, you have to help us. And there were people just lying on the floor.

At around 11:30 p.m., Christelle was ready to deliver her baby. Baby John was born. I just remember crying so much. Then I said I'm sorry, I can't do more, I really need to leave now. And I did.'

Stephanie took a cab back home. Her place was no more. It was completely wrecked.

'I grabbed my passport, got into the car and drove to my parents. I cried all the way. Why did I get to live? That's not fair. Why did I live when so many others died? Why did mothers have to be traumatized in what should have been the most beautiful day of their lives?

'One thing helps me get over this. That is knowing that literally so many were taking their last breath while I helped two babies come to life that day.'

Stephanie moved back to Australia in October 2021 where she is working as an Ob-gyn.

PART TWO

The Myth of Resilience

The Lebanese have endured decades of volatility and bloodshed. They are often dubbed as 'resilient', but that is only a myth.

In reality, the Lebanese are not resilient. Resilience implies overcoming a misfortune, rebuilding a country around sane and healthy principles, finding solutions, freeing oneself from an oppressor, adapting but to better conditions. Instead, the Lebanese are just adjusting to an impossible way of life, unable to create better alternatives. They are today an exhausted and traumatized people, conforming to a life of subsistence. They never healed their wounds or recovered from their traumas, including after 15 years of civil war. They never really broke free from the shackles of a corrupt political class or from foreign interference.Resilience is a myth, if not a lie, that politicians coaxed them into believing, to encourage them to keep on going in unacceptable circumstances. That myth also serves the interests of the ruling elite and consolidates their power. The politicians are resilient, not the people.The women's stories transcend that myth and paint a reality of protracted violence and trauma that seem to have no end. Lebanon's history appears to repeat itself. Its people are never safe and have not healed or moved on. Theirs is a life of survival.

5

Lebanon: A Dysfunctional Compromise

It is impossible to comprehend Lebanon's current collapse without understanding its past. Yes, Lebanon is undergoing its worst economic and financial crisis ever, but the roots of its problems are not only economic. Lebanon's main problem is one of governance. To understand some of the historical events mentioned by the women in this book, it is essential that I try to explain, although briefly, how Lebanon's history of political compromise and foreign interference, combined with its sectarian elements, political system, and of course corruption, are factors in its demise.

Lebanon's history, ancient and modern, has always been shaped by foreign interests. Internal divisions, political compromises, and the country's geography have allowed such meddling to intrude, survive, and thrive. For much of their history, the Lebanese people themselves – different interest groups and political opportunists – have sought the help of foreign powers, destabilizing and weakening the country in the process.

When I look back over the decades and centuries of my country, it is Lebanon's identity that has always been in question, dividing the Lebanese since before the birth of their modern nation and turning the country into a fertile ground for proxy wars. We Lebanese have not to this day come to grips with our identity crisis. We don't agree on our past, present or future. Depending on who you ask, a Lebanese person will tell you a different story about who they are, what their origins are, and how they see Lebanon and its future. We can't even agree on who is a martyr, a friend, or an opponent. Even Lebanon's foreign policy is schizophrenic, with rival political leaders befriending each other's foes and allies.

When a country seems so vulnerable on the inside, and sits on a regional seismic fault line on the outside, it is bound to shake all the time.

THE EMIRATE OF MOUNT LEBANON: BETWEEN OTTOMAN OPPRESSION AND EUROPEAN INFLUENCE

The beginnings of Lebanon as a modern nation are usually traced back to the sixteenth century. Lebanon was known as the Emirate of Mount Lebanon under the Ottoman Empire – a huge empire which included much of the Middle East and Eastern Europe and was ruled from Constantinople. Geographically, within the Emirate was the central part of today's Lebanon. It consisted of a group of religious communities, namely persecuted Maronite Christians and Druze, who sought shelter and settled on its land. The Emirate, so called because it was ruled by an 'Emir' – or ruler – appointed by the Ottomans, was not an autonomous entity. It obeyed the Ottomans.

From 1516 to 1840 all attempts to form an independent nation without direct Ottoman rule were crushed. Western nations had no direct interest in the region, although that would change with time.

Starting in 1840, the schism between Mount Lebanon's two main religious communities, the Druze and the Maronites, began to widen. Western powers also became more interested in exploiting Mount Lebanon and the wider region.

With time, the Maronites grew closer to the French and the Druze to the British Empire. Russia was also increasingly playing the role of a protector for the Christian Orthodox minority who lived in the Emirate. Missionaries proliferated in Mount Lebanon to promote the interests of competing Western empires under the guise of religion. These powers were now advocating for a new political system for the Emirate, one that was more autonomous from the Ottoman Empire.

In 1842 and following a first rift between the Maronites and the Druzes, Mount Lebanon was divided into two political entities, known as Qaimaqamiatain. A northern district was given to the Maronites and a southern one for the Druze. It was the first attempt to organize Mount Lebanon politically and more 'autonomously' from the Ottomans. The new structure, fostered by the West, fed further the divisions between the two sects. Violent conflict between the Druze and the Maronites erupted as early as 1845.

The year 1860 would mark a turning point in the history of Mount Lebanon. Both Druzes and Maronites fell prey to the competing interests of European empires. Christian peasants organized an uprising against their feudal landowners and their privileges, supported by France and the Lebanese clergy. Fearing the spread of the revolt into their territory, the Druze, supported by the Ottomans and the British, opposed the uprising, labelling it as a Christian uprising that threatens their power and existence. The grievances between the two communities were deepening, especially because the Christians started outnumbering the Druzes and were starting to gain political power. Druze peasants were armed as a reaction. The conflict culminated in massacres between Druzes and Christians and marked Lebanon's first sectarian war. France intervened, ostensibly to stop the killings of the Christians at the hands of the Druzes, who ended winning the war.

Following that violent episode, an agreement was signed between the Ottomans, Austria, Prussia, Great Britain, and Russia to dispatch European soldiers, half of them French, in an attempt to restore order. The agreement also paved the way for a change in the political system.

The year 1861 marked the birth of Lebanon's first autonomous polity and confessional political system known as Mutasarifiya. A foreign Christian governor appointed by the Ottomans headed the Mutasarifiya in tandem with a local council representing the main religious sects. Lebanon's state started taking shape after 1861, but the polity was far from being sovereign, in truth the Ottomans were still in charge.

THE BIRTH OF GREATER LEBANON: A EUROPEAN COMPROMISE FOR A CONFESSIONAL LEBANON

When I reflect on Lebanon's birth as a modern nation, I think of a caesarean section operated by Western powers on a fragile body, one that had endured 400 years of Ottoman occupation. Essentially, Lebanon as we know it was a concession from Europeans to sectarian leaders, who agreed to share power through an insidious confessional system.

The creation of modern Lebanon known as the Greater Lebanon in 1920 was as a result of Franco–British colonial partition of the Middle East after the end of the First World War and the disintegration of the Ottoman Empire. Lebanon was a gift to France. Its new boundaries were imposed by the West though they also reflected the aspirations of some Lebanese, mainly the Church and some Christian groups. To use the words of the Lebanese historian Fawaz Traboulsi, 'Greater Lebanon's creation was mainly determined by the interests of France in dividing and controlling Syria, in the context of the partition of the Arab provinces of the ex-Ottoman Empire between Paris and London.'

The new Lebanon expanded from its original size, to include in addition to Mount Lebanon the coastal cities of Beirut, Tripoli in the north, Tyre and Saida in the south, and the Bekaa Valley in the east. It was now comprised of large Sunni and Shiite Muslim communities in addition to the existing Christian and Druze. Throughout its mandate over Lebanon, France relied mostly on the Christian Maronites.

The young nation was increasingly divided between two camps: one, mostly Christian, which believed in Lebanon as a democratic nation under French tutelage, and another, mainly Sunni, which believed in Lebanon's place in the Arab nationalist camp and in its historical unity with Syria. The two movements would be known as Lebanism versus Arabism and would shape the country's politics for decades.

The two competing camps, under the auspices of Egypt and the blessing of Western powers, reached a compromise in 1942 to prevent armed conflict. The compromise was known as the National Pact. It was an unwritten informal agreement reached between the country's two main sects, the Sunnis and Maronites, whereby the Christians renounced protection from France and the Muslims renounced their aspiration for unity with Syria. In return, both sides would get guarantees in terms of political representation. The pact laid the foundation of Lebanon's modern political confessionalism and stated that the three key government positions of president, prime minister, and parliament speaker were to be held respectively by a Maronite Christian, a Sunni Muslim, and a Shia Muslim. Parliament would also be divided among the different confessions based on a population census from 1932. No official demographic census has taken place since.

Starting in 1941, and with France weakened by German occupation, pressure mounted internally and externally, namely through the British, for independence. In November 1943, Lebanon's parliament amended the constitution ending the French mandate. France briefly detained Lebanon's leaders before succumbing to local demands and international pressure. Lebanon gained its independence on 22 November. The last of the French soldiers left in 1946. The country was free, but its colonial scars would endure.

POST-INDEPENDENCE: COLD WAR INTERESTS
AND ARAB NATIONALISM

Lebanon witnessed a period of relative stability and prosperity following independence. From the 1950s to 1975 it benefited from an oil boom in the Gulf region, with Arab capital flowing into its banks after a wave of nationalizations in Egypt, Syria, and Iraq. After the creation of the state of Israel in 1948, Palestinian businessmen also moved their capital and expertise to Lebanon. The country became a centre for commerce and banking as its economy started to focus on services and finance. In addition, it was an important tourism hub in the region. But this period also planted the seeds of conflict and paved the way for a protracted conflict a few decades later.

Lebanon's identity crisis and instability were reignited in the context of the Cold War. The country was caught between a pro-American camp and a pro-Arab and Soviet camp. These divisions led to the modern nation's first brief civil war in 1958. The conflict came at the peak of the Cold War and reflected the tension within the country between the mainly Sunni pan-Arab nationalist movement close to Egypt's popular President Gamal Abdel Nasser and the Soviets, and the mainly Christian camp of President Camille Chamoun close to the United States and the West.

The US marines intervened at the behest of Chamoun with a landing on Beirut's shores on 15 July 1958 dubbed 'Operation Blue Bat'. Lebanon was of strategic importance for the United States in its wider containment plan to restrain the Soviets. Arab nationalism was seen as a threat. Once again, Lebanon was a site of occupation for the great powers.

ISRAEL, PALESTINIAN RESISTANCE AND THE
PRELUDE TO THE CIVIL WAR

The creation of Israel in 1948 had lasting ramifications for Lebanon and the region. As early as 1949, Lebanon took in about 100,000 Palestinian refugees who had fled or been expelled from their homes after the creation of the Jewish state. Their numbers would increase with the years and their settlement in Lebanon created opportunities for armed Palestinian resistance groups which operated from Lebanon against Israel. Their military operations would further divide the Lebanese, especially after 1967 and the defeat of the Arabs against Israel in the so-called Six-Day War. The Cairo Agreement signed between the Palestinian Liberation Authority and Lebanon in 1969 would legitimize Palestinian guerrilla resistance from Lebanese soil, paving the way for the civil war in 1975.

Although there is a common belief that the civil war was triggered by the Palestinians' operation against Israel from Lebanon and the opposition of many Lebanese to it, this was in no way the sole or root cause of the war, which persisted even after the Palestinian military activities ceased in 1982. Lingering and pre-existing issues, such as the power-sharing agreement between the different sects in Lebanon since 1943 and the country's relations with its neighbours and the world, have played a role in fuelling the conflict as well. The war was not just a sectarian conflict between Christians and Muslims; that would be a naïve, simplistic assumption. Although the demarcation lines seem to have been around that divide, the Lebanese kept shifting alliances internally and externally throughout the war. During the war's 15 years, there were bouts of intra-Shia fighting, and even intra-Christian wars between 1988 and 1990. The civil war was also definitely not just a war of the others, as some would describe it. It did involve too many countries and actors and revolved around external issues including the Israeli–Palestinian conflict, the Cold War, Arab nationalism, but it was also feeding on sectarianism and old grievances. For 15 years, regional conflicts and ideologies intersected and clashed with local divisions and issues.

THE BIRTH OF HEZBOLLAH AND SYRIA'S OCCUPATION OF LEBANON

The civil war in Lebanon led to two more major foreign occupations of the country. The first was in 1976, when Syrian troops intervened against the Palestinians at the demand of the Lebanese Christians. The troops would stay in Lebanon until 2005.

In 1978 and 1982, Israel invaded Lebanon. Its forces stayed in the country until 2000. Its second occupation in 1982 opened the way for Iran's influence in the country and the birth of Hezbollah, an Iranian-backed militia that would organize a major guerrilla operation against Israel in Lebanon before turning into a major armed political player after the war. Hezbollah was the only militia from the civil war not to disarm after the war under the pretext of resisting Israeli occupation in the south of Lebanon. Even after Israel's pullout in 2000, Hezbollah continued to claim legitimacy for its military arsenal and considers itself the main representative of Lebanon's Shiite community. Ever since, it has been a part of every government and considered by some to be even stronger than the state.

The Lebanese protracted conflict that started in 1975 terminated in 1990. I was only five years old when it ended. I don't remember much from the war because I was too young and lived in the north of Lebanon where there was no fighting those years. But I do recall that in the very last years of the conflict, my grandparents and my cousins moved to our home town in the north and lived there briefly. I also remember Syrian army checkpoints everywhere, including a military camp where I saw soldiers train every single morning on my way to school. But that's it. My knowledge of the civil war, like most of those born at the end of or during the post-war era, is based on stories I heard from my grandmother and parents, on books I have made the effort to read, on movies I have watched. The civil war is not taught at school. Lebanon's official history books end in 1943 and have not been updated. Political leaders have not agreed on or worked on a common history project that can be used in the national curriculum. We have no collective memory of the war as Lebanese. We were forced into a collective amnesia instead. Our recollections are different and we have different perspectives on the conflict, its cause, its end. What you read here is based on my own knowledge, which I have accumulated through my research as a journalist.

The end of the civil war was marked by a peace deal in 1989 and known as the Taif Agreement, after the Saudi Arabian city where it was signed. Taif marked a temporary truce more than a permanent peace solution. Mediated by the League of Arab States led by Saudi Arabia, whose role in Lebanon had grown in the 1970s, and Syria, it failed to resolve the root causes of the conflict including Lebanon's identity crisis and political sectarianism. The presence of Syrian forces on Lebanese soil, Israel's occupation of Lebanese land, and Hezbollah's status as an armed militia were also not resolved. The first president elected after the Taif Agreement, René Mouawad, who is from my home town and my family, was assassinated in a car bomb just 17 days after taking office. His murder on 22 November 1989 is something I recall vividly, though I was barely four. My paternal grandmother, who lived with us, was watching my brother and I that afternoon, and I can still remember how much she panicked and wept when she heard the news on the TV. The assassinated president had walked my mother to the altar on her wedding day.

The war ended but Lebanon's warlords remained in power and managed to secure an amnesty for themselves, through a general amnesty law, yet there was never a full national reconciliation. There was no effort to find out the truth, or to find justice for the victims.

The fate of those who disappeared in the war is still unknown. Lebanese women have been leading a long fight to discover what happened to their loved ones, but to no avail.

The Taif Agreement made Syria Lebanon's powerbroker and cemented its military presence in Lebanon. Syria was awarded power in Lebanon after it took sides with the United States during the 1990 Gulf War. Under the helm of Hafiz al-Assad, then his son Bashar al-Assad, Syria would occupy Lebanon and become deeply involved in its political and economic affairs as well as its foreign policy, further eroding the country's already fragile sovereignty.

An alliance between Lebanon's political elite and Syria thrived in the post-war era, with Lebanon's politicians sharing the post-war reconstruction pie with their occupier. Syria's occupation of Lebanon would last until 2005. My own father was a member of parliament during the last five years of the occupation. He was coerced into many decisions and threatened before he finally joined forces with those opposing the Syrian hegemony.

Resistance against Syria started building up in 2000 after Israel's withdrawal from Lebanon. It was made official in 2004 with UN resolution 1559, sponsored by the French and the Americans, and calling for the 'disbanding and disarmament of all militias', in reference to Hezbollah backed by Syria and Iran. It affirmed Lebanon's sovereignty in relation to Syria's occupation.

The price of resolution 1559 that spelled the end of Syrian troops' presence in Lebanon was the assassination of Rafik Hariri on 14 February 2005. The former prime minister, who had both Lebanese and Saudi nationality and represented Saudi interests in Lebanon, had started distancing himself from Syria and openly supported resolution 1559 in 2004.

After Hariri's assassination in a car bomb in 2005, many Lebanese, myself included, took to the streets demanding that Syrian troops leave Lebanon. The protest movement would be known as the 'Cedar Revolution'. Syria, facing increasing international pressure, pulled its troops out of Lebanon in 2005, but in reality its occupation has never ended. To this day it maintains an influence through its intelligence apparatus and political allies. Lebanon was once again divided between two camps, this time between those who sought an end to Syrian occupation and wanted Hezbollah to disarm, and those who didn't.

A POWER-SHARING SYSTEM AT THE SERVICE OF LEBANON'S SECTARIAN LEADERS

Lebanon's sectarian power-sharing system, created in 1943, has survived ever since. Initially an informal agreement within the

National Pact, it became enshrined in the constitution at the end of the civil war, though with amendments. The system might seem at first glance a fair representation of Lebanon's various sects. But it has actually proved with time to be extremely dysfunctional, weakening the state and allowing narrow sectarian and communal interests to take precedence over national ones. The sectarian power-sharing system prospered under Syria's tutelage, and with it thrived sectarian corruption. For many Lebanese, the ruling elite seems to have built a patronage network using governmental institutions such as ministries as resources offering services to their constituencies in return for political allegiance. They create unnecessary posts in the civil service and 'ghost jobs' within various public institutions in return for loyalty.

With the end of Syria's military role in Lebanon, the country's confessional power-sharing system became even more dysfunctional. The arbiter was gone and Lebanon remained deeply divided. A complex form of decision-making was put in place by the political elite whereby decisions at the Cabinet level could not be taken without broad consensus between various parties. It was a way to retain the balance of power and protect their vested interests.

This has had the effect of disabling reforms and effective economic policies and worsening the political deadlock. Forming governments also became a nightmare, with political parties continuously delaying as they bickered over their share of the pie.

This book is about women and for women, so it is important to highlight here how much the Lebanese sectarian system has also had a detrimental impact on them. The stories in this book are a witness to that. Lebanese women are second-class citizens and will remain so as long as that system is in place.

Lebanon's confessional system has created a gender apartheid. All personal status matters like marriage, divorce, child custody, and inheritance, continue to be under the control of religious courts which are controlled by men and discriminate against women. There is no unified civil code in Lebanon for personal-status affairs but rather 15 separate personal-status laws and courts in the country for the 18 different recognized religious communities. Therefore, women are subjected to sexist laws within these courts not just regarding men from their religion but also regarding other women from other religions. My rights as a Catholic woman are not the same as the rights of women from other confessions.

SYRIA'S CONFLICT AND ITS SPILLOVER INTO LEBANON: EMBOLDENING HEZBOLLAH AT THE EXPENSE OF STATE INSTITUTIONS

The Syrian uprising in 2011 that descended into a civil war had deep economic and political spillover effects on Lebanon.

More than a million refugees flocked into the country, which was already suffering from a weak infrastructure. Cross-border trade was severely affected, tourism and foreign investment dwindled. Hezbollah's involvement in the conflict in support of the Syrian regime further aggravated the impact of the war. Gulf states, which supported the anti-Assad forces and felt threatened by Iran's growing influence in the region, punished Lebanon for Hezbollah's role in the Syrian conflict by taking their dollars out of the country, issuing a travel ban on their own nationals, and halting their investments in Lebanon. Hezbollah's role in Syria also led to a political deadlock in Lebanon, which was now deeply divided between a pro-Syria and pro-Hezbollah camp, and those opposed to them. The explosion in Beirut on 4 August 2020, based on the evidence we have today, epitomizes the spillover into Lebanon of Syria's war and Hezbollah's involvement in it.

This short history is vital to this book, because Lebanon's collapse did not happen overnight: it has been brewing for decades. It was the work of its political class, but it was also in some ways the inevitable fate of a country whose birth and survival were the result of a dysfunctional compromise between local and foreign powers. Lebanon's civil war has in some ways never ended, and the country continues to remain a hostage to competing visions regarding its role in the region and the world. Our history keeps repeating itself, because we have still not broken free from corrupt leaders or their international political allies. Lebanon has still not settled on a defined national identity, and its people are still looking for the nationhood they never had.

6

History Repeats Itself

SALWA BAALBAKI

*'The moment I spot him, it's a flashback. I am
taken back to a moment from the civil war.'*

How much trauma can one bear in a lifetime?

It's a question I keep asking myself after having lived in and
reported for so many years from Lebanon and the Middle East. I
am just staggered by the level of violence that we have endured and
tolerated, over and again.

Salwa and I had never met before. The owner of the daily
newspaper where she worked, *An-Nahar*, Lebanon's oldest and
once most-renowned daily, put me in touch with her after I read a
Facebook post of hers that caught my attention. Salwa seemed a bit
hesitant about the interview when I reached out on the phone, but
she eventually agreed to see me.

We met once at the paper's headquarters in downtown Beirut,
almost a year after the explosion. Salwa took me into a private
office overlooking the street, its windows still covered with wooden
panels. The building's facades had still not been replaced. It was
noisy in the room and I could barely hear her. She spoke in a soft
but croaky voice.

Salwa had joined *An-Nahar* back in 2004. This was a year before the assassination of Gibran Tueni, the newspaper's editor.

'I worked with him for about a year before he was killed.'

Tueni, an outspoken journalist against Syria's post-civil war occupation of Lebanon, was murdered in a car bomb on the outskirts of Beirut in December 2005. I was still a student at the American University of Beirut that year and Lebanon was caught in a vortex of political assassinations, mostly car bombs, that targeted and killed politicians who were advocating for Syria's departure from Lebanon, including the late prime minister, Rafik Hariri. The bombings also targeted intelligence officers who were investigating Hariri's murder. The political assassinations would last until 2013, and many civilians lost their lives.

In mid-August 2020, two weeks after the Beirut explosion, a UN-backed international tribunal found three men with links to Hezbollah guilty of the assassination of Hariri. But they were tried in absentia and remain at large. The tribunal, while it recognized that Hezbollah and the Syrian regime had an incentive to eliminate Hariri, had insufficient proof to hold either side responsible.

Between 2013 and 2015, explosions rocked the city of Tripoli in the north of Lebanon, having targeted two mosques. Various bombings also targeted residential areas in the Beirut suburbs, where Salwa lived, killing scores of civilians. The Islamic State group (ISIS) claimed responsibility for these latter attacks, which were believed to be linked to Hezbollah's involvement in the Syrian conflict. The Lebanese armed militia was backing the Syrian regime militarily.

'When I walk on the street, I don't feel safe. When a car passes by, I imagine it might be loaded with explosives and it's going to detonate.'

Salwa has survived a lot of violence: the civil war, Israel's wars in Lebanon, and the bombings in the suburbs where she lives. Despite all the trauma she'd suffered, she was not ready for 4 August 2020.

That day, Salwa was working from home because of the pandemic. But she came to the office in the afternoon to submit a story on Lebanon's economic crisis, which she had been working on for the launch of *An-Nahar*'s new Arabic website.

'I finished it and I remember telling my editor that I feel like something is about to happen, and I just wanted to submit the story and get it done with. I swear I said that.'

But Salwa never had time to hand in her story.

'I remember waking up and standing by the wall. I saw that my arm was injured but I looked at it only once because I was too scared. It was a deep wound. My hand was barely holding on to my arm. The tendons and ligaments of my wrist were all gone, torn. I had to hold it with my other hand. I just couldn't look again. I never looked at it until after the surgery.'

Salwa paused. Her voice cracked. She was shaking.

'I stood idle by the wall waiting for the second air strike because I remember hearing Israeli jets before the explosion, that is what I heard. I know their sound all too well. I have survived many of Israel's wars in Lebanon.'

The narrative of the airplanes is one I gathered from almost every single survivor interviewed for this book. I also remember hearing that sound myself. But forensic experts have linked that roar to the intensity of the fire and the combustion of oxygen and chemicals in the air, as well as to the smaller explosions preceding the blast. There has been no credible evidence to this day documenting an air strike or even the sight of jets.

'I was standing and waiting for my death, then someone shouted "Salwa, you are bleeding to death, come here." I still can't remember who it was. We were literally in open space, everything was gone. If I was not standing by the wall, I would have fallen off the building. Only the columns were standing.

'I walk on the debris and towards a colleague, his name is Khalil. The moment I spot him, it's a flashback. I am taken back to a moment from the civil war. I was a young girl, a man was sitting the exact same way, we were outside our house in the south and he was injured. He was crouching and bleeding to death. He was sitting the exact same way, the same way as Khalil, and screaming "God, where do I go now!" It was the exact same scene. Horrifying.'

This was Salwa's account that I read on Facebook, which made me want to talk to her. It was the testimony of a generation of women with lingering trauma and no proper healing. One traumatic event took Salwa back to another.

'I told Khalil to stand up so we can leave. He asks me where the staircase was, he was new at the newspaper. I had no clue. I couldn't recognize anything. The whole place had changed. I remember someone helped me go down, the stairs were covered in blood.'

Salwa gasped.

'I reached the entrance, I saw a woman knocked on the floor, her face down, she looked dead, oh God.'

Salwa paused, then started crying. She looked so vulnerable. I was sitting across a table from her. She went on.

'They took me out. Outside was an apocalypse. I kept wondering what Israel wanted, why, what's in here for Israel to bomb us like that. I live in the Beirut suburbs and in 2006 Israel bombed our street. It all came back to me, the destruction, the smashed buildings, it all looked the same.'

Salwa was referring to the second Israeli–Lebanese war, known as the July war of 2006. Israel, following a Hezbollah operation on the border that had killed three Israeli soldiers and captured two, carried out thousands of air strikes on Lebanon, including on Beirut's suburbs where Salwa lived. More than 1,100 Lebanese died, mostly civilians. That was a summer I will never forget.

'There was a massacre inside,' continued Salwa, referring to a hospital she was taken to on 4 August 2020. 'People moaning, people dying.'

She sobbed. I felt paralysed every time that happened in an interview. As a journalist, I could only give these women some space, a respite.

'They made me sit on a chair and there was a little boy next to me, he was maybe 10, he was alone and was badly injured in the head, and he looked like he was staring into void. He was alive but looked like he was dead. He was losing consciousness and every time he closed his eyes; my heart would drop. I tried to keep him awake. Please stay with me, I would beg him. I was later told that someone found him on the street and brought him to the hospital. They couldn't reach his mother. He broke my heart.'

She paused, then sighed.

'I have been through many wars. When I am sitting alone, and it's peaceful, I hear the sound of explosions. I survived the explosion of Bir el-Abed that targeted Sayyed Mohammad Hussein Fadlallah, and it left its mark on me.'

In 1985, as the civil war was raging, a car bomb exploded in Beirut near the house of the Shia cleric Sayyed Mohammad Hussein Fadlallah. The bombing, a failed assassination attempt, killed 80 people, almost all of them civilians.

'My parents were abroad and I was a teenager. I was in a grocery shop and everything collapsed on me. There were many young girls who perished that day, so many. I think they were praying nearby.'

Salwa kept talking about the civil war. I felt like that was all she wanted to talk about. Not the explosion, but the past it had brought back. Maybe that was her coping mechanism: talking about the endless and unhealed trauma she'd survived throughout her life.

'There is another story I can't forget from the war. We were staying with a Christian family, they felt protected by our presence from the Palestinians and we, as Muslims, found protection in their house from the Christian militias. I remember one day, Christian militias started raiding the area, and there was a guy, his name was Elias, who told us to stand by the window and say we were peaceful Lebanese civilians. I remember we were crying and saying that out loud, repeating it and crying, these were horrible moments, moments that never leave me. Christian militia men came inside and took us out and ordered us to stand by a wall, I remember it so well. They separated us into Christians and Muslims. They were fighting among each other on who to kill first. Then they decided to take us as hostages. My uncle had connections, he saved us and took us to another house before we moved to the south. But that moment of standing on the wall is something I will never forget. It always comes back to me.'

More than 100,000 people lost their lives in Lebanon's civil war, about 20,000 are still unaccounted for, and close to two-thirds of the population were displaced. I ask Salwa if the civil war was worse, since she seemed to bring it up a lot.

'No. The civil war was somehow gradual, there were phases, it prepared you. This blast felt like the civil war entirely came together and exploded, in an instant. You saw everything destroyed in a second.

'I don't sleep well at night. My colleagues used to make fun of me for sleeping early, now I go to bed at 3 a.m. I am not happy. I used to be a happy person, now nothing makes me happy. I haven't laughed since August 4th. I am always crying, anything makes me cry. I don't know how I didn't die, it's weird, it's a miracle. You saw our building, the destruction, how didn't we die? I was removing pieces of glass from my hair for more than a week.'

I ask her if as a journalist she knows anything I don't about what happened on 4 August. She smiles, in a sarcastic way.

'No one knows what happened. Ammonium nitrate blew up, but who got it here? Who kept it? There was the hypothesis that Israel was behind this, but I no longer believe it was. Everyone should be questioned. This is the crime of our times, everyone should help with the investigation. You know what I would like to see? All of them, all of those responsible for the blast, put together somewhere and blown up. This is how much hatred I have.

'I have no hope in this country anymore, I am still here because I need to take care of my father. Everything disgusts me. The corruption, the way politicians deal with people, it is disgusting. They don't care. But we are to blame.

'I want to leave this country although I love it so much. I have the right to live. I really want to leave. I wish my dad would leave but he is old now and he is attached to the land here. I can't leave him. But the fear of war never leaves me.'

DALAL EL ADM

'I spent my life fleeing something.'

Dalal's daughter died alone in her apartment in Beirut on 4 August. She was 37.

Krystel took her last breath after calling her father, from under the rubble, begging him to help. Her last words to him were: 'Dad save me. Please save me.'

But it was too late.

Dalal and I met in her apartment in Jounieh, a city north of Beirut. She had turned the place into a memorial for her daughter with photos of Krystel plastered all over the walls of the apartment, nestled amid candles and photos of saints.

'I used to live where Krystel lived, it is my parents' house. It was a beautiful old Lebanese house with high ceilings and ornate arcades. The house resisted all the bombings during the civil war. The shells, the mortars. I have an emotional attachment to it. She decorated the place, including a bedroom for her father and I. Krystel lived there because it was too far for her to commute to work from here every day.'

Dalal's house was only 20 kilometres away from Beirut, but with Lebanon's chronic traffic jams, due to the lack of public transportation, bad roads, and an ever-increasing number of cars, the commute could last more than an hour.

'I called her at noon to see if she'll come for lunch. She said she was coming around 4:30 p.m. I prepared escalope and fries, her favourite, and I waited for her.'

Instead of driving from work straight to her parents that afternoon, Krystel decided to check on a little orphan whom she had been taking care of.

'She bought him a laptop and gave money to his grandmother. She called me saying they were so happy. Then she passed by the house in Gemmayzeh. I didn't know she was there. I was waiting for her.

'I heard airplanes, I opened the windows. I turned on the television. I saw that there was an explosion but I didn't know what happened. I thought Krystel was on her way here. I called her, she didn't reply.'

Dalal sobbed. I was trying to stay calm. I had known Krystel since we were kids. Dalal was a friend of my maternal aunt and her daughter was my cousin's childhood best friend.

'I always protected my children. I always told them the good things about Lebanon. I hid the war and its hardship inside me. We lived our life with bombs and attacks. I spent my life fleeing something.

'When I think about the past, all I can remember is us carrying things and running away. In 1976 we left Beirut. We moved to the mountains. I got married in 1977 and we left the country. My husband studied medicine in Brussels, he stayed there for 15 years. He was specializing in cardiology in a medical centre. But he always wanted to move back to Lebanon. He had hope in Lebanon. I gave birth to one child in Brussels and the others here. Krystel was born in Lebanon in 1984 amidst the war. She was a white baby shining like a crystal. Despite the violence, I didn't let my children feel anything, I stayed strong for them. I tried my best to keep a sense of normalcy for them. I never broke down in front of them. I had to stand up for my family.'

Lebanese and Arab mothers silently carry a heavy load throughout their lives and keep going for the sake of their kids. They lose themselves to their children. Such was the case of my grandmother who sacrificed her life for her children. They are also mothers who raise us amid conflict but do their utmost best to establish a sense of normalcy in our lives, to shield us from the reality around us. Such was the case of my mother, who went to great lengths to make us feel safe and provided us with a lifestyle that is not typical of a country trapped in violence and instability.

'We stayed in Lebanon until 1989 before fleeing again. We left because one day the kids were playing outside on the swings. Five minutes later, a missile fell on the swings. We left afterwards. My husband Nazih stayed, his patients were here and he was tired of starting over and over again. I left with the kids, first to Brussels then to Pau, in Belgium. I was alone with three kids. I cannot even describe how difficult it was. It was a huge responsibility. And in Lebanon the situation was getting worse.'

Dalal eventually moved back to Lebanon after the civil war ended in 1990. Krystel went to school there and only left the country fifteen years later, to pursue her graduate studies in finance in France.

I asked Dalal why Krystel eventually came back to Beirut.

'She came back when banks here were thriving, she got a good job offer from a bank here. They were recruiting a lot of Lebanese living abroad. She wanted to be close to her family and friends. She came back after nine years abroad.'

I found it ironic that Krystel came back to work for the banks that robbed us of our savings, so they could finance a corrupt government that ended up killing her.

Dalal paused. I wondered if she regretted supporting Krystel's decision to return home.

'This is our destiny. I'm a believer and I think it's good that Krystel was a good person. She was a good Christian. But I don't know why this happened. Why were there explosives next to our home? And all this nitrate they stored in one area? During the civil war, the wheat silos of the port didn't move, when Israel bombed, they didn't move. Now they are gone. Our government killed us and a part of me is dead.'

As we were chatting, her husband came in. He was in pyjamas though it was almost noon, and he looked tired. He shyly said hello and quickly retreated. I asked her how he was doing. I had heard he stopped practising medicine after his daughter's death. It must have been so difficult for him. Krystel had called her father for help from underneath the rubble, but he had been unable to save her.

'He's broken, we are all broken. We try to stay strong but we are not. I live with her. Look at all these pictures.'

Dalal stood up and we walked around the room, looking at the numerous photos, giant posters, small framed images, religious relics, prayers on wooden boards with photos of Krystel on them.

'She used to send me a lot of photos when she was abroad. Look at how beautiful she was.'

Despite everything that Lebanon had taken away from her, Dalal, her husband, and Krystel's friends started a foundation in her name. Dalal channelled her grief and energy into her daughter's foundation, the Krystel El Adm Foundation. She said it was her only solace.

'We want to keep her legacy alive. We are focusing on education. We have helped more than thirty families pay for their children's school tuitions this year (in 2021), about 120 students. We also distribute food, kids need to eat well to do well at school.'

Lebanon's food inflation was the highest in 2022, according to the World Bank. Soaring prices have left most of the nation's population food insecure. Every time I go grocery shopping when I am there, I wonder how people put food on their table every day. Prices are insane, more expensive than Paris, and the quality is not even comparable. Most goods on supermarket shelves are not the same anymore and have been replaced with lesser-quality equivalents. In restaurants, the physical menu never shows prices as they constantly change. You have to scan a digital barcode to see the latest ones.

'Children also need books. We give those,' adds Dalal. 'Krystel wanted children to have a bright future. When she gave a laptop to that young boy on August 4th, before her death, it was so he can do online classes. She always pushed him, she told him if he studied, he would be a director one day. Those were her last words to him.'

Nothing scares me more than the collapse of Lebanon's education system. The economic crisis dealt the education sector a heavy blow. As I am writing these lines in early 2023, public sector teachers have been on strike because their salaries were too low and so children have not been in school for months. Enrolment in schools dropped from 60 per cent in the 2020–21 academic year to 43 per cent in 2021–22, according to the UN, and 'more than 4 in 10 youth in Lebanon reduced spending on education to buy basic food, medicine and other essential items'. Many students were moved from private to public schools because of dwindling purchasing power and higher tuition fees. But public schools, which were already under-funded before the crisis, are not even functioning properly. There are no lights in the classrooms because of the power shortage and the rising price of fuel.

In higher education, the situation is also dire. Over the past two years, I have received tons of messages from undergraduate students seeking help to be able to continue attending university. Many teachers have also left the country. The quality of education itself has been affected. Prestigious universities like the American University of Beirut are now opening branches abroad to keep their institution afloat after losing so many students and professors.

For a country once hailed for its education system and skilled workers, Lebanon now risks raising a lost generation. Krystel's foundation work is crucial and it keeps Dalal going. The grieving mother is trying to find a purpose and some meaning in the absurd departure of her young daughter.

'We lived through a lot during the civil war. Forty years since it ended, but the war is not over. It never ended. We are moving backwards every day, there's nothing worse than this. I used to compare myself to Palestinians and think that at least if I left, I still had a country to go back to, I still have a land. But now it feels like that has also been taken away from us. It is our duty to protect this land.'

History repeats itself for Dalal but she is still not giving up. She decided to stay and fight.

7

Survival

SIHAM TAKIAN

*'I had diarrhoea once, just diarrhoea, and I could
not find anything to cure it. We live in hell.'*

Siham like most Lebanese is not living, she is surviving.

She survived the Beirut blast on top of a wave of economic
violence that no human being should have to endure in the twenty-
first century. Lebanon's economic collapse has been described by
the World Bank as one of the world's worst economic crises since
the 1850s, and that is definitely no exaggeration.

I covered the Venezuelan economic crisis and its ensuing refugee
exodus in 2019 from neighbouring Colombia and was shocked by
some of the stories I reported on. I remember this single mother
with six children, her name was Maria. She had to sell the roof of
her house in Venezuela in return for shoes, so she and her children
could walk all the way to Colombia. Her roof was the only valuable
thing she had left. The Venezuelan currency was worthless. Maria
could no longer afford food and medicine. She had to leave.

I never imagined that my people would suffer from a similar
unfathomable economic crisis. Less than a year after my trip to
South America, this would also become the story of Lebanon.

I met Siham in 2021. We were both featured in a national women's campaign in 2020 highlighting the stories of '16 heroic women who provide safety to people around them, even though they don't feel safe themselves'.

Siham owned a small deli shop in Mar Mikhael in Beirut, where she sat every day for long hours behind a small wooden desk, selling canned food, cigarettes, and beverages. She cared for her sick husband, as well as her brother and his wife. She had no children.

She was 63 but looked much older. Her hardship weighed heavily on her large body and her mind. She looked tired and irritated but still managed to be kind. People who came to her shop were mostly regulars. They actually came because she was there. She called everyone 'habibi' ('my love'), and she called me 'Dalloul'.

Siham's kindness extended to the little animals around her. She was known as the cat lady. Despite being in need herself, she would feed the neighbourhood cats every single day. They congregated in her shop and slept on its shelves.

'People think I pay for the cats' food, they make fun of me, they say I am rich I can feed them,' she said as she opened a can of food for three cats. I couldn't help but notice that Siham was almost toothless. I could only see one tooth when she spoke.

'There is a pets' organization that came to me after the explosion. They saw how many cats I was feeding and they saw I was injured. They give me money every month to buy them food. People also donate. I love these cats. They keep me company. Imagine, the government did not ask about me, but there were organizations who looked after the cats in the city.'

Siham had severe cuts in her legs due to the explosion and could not walk normally anymore. Glass had torn through the veins of her foot. She needed surgery and physical therapy to rehabilitate it, but could not afford any.

Both her house and her shop were also damaged in the explosion and yet Siham did not get any form of official aid or support.

'My shop withstood thirty years of war. The civil war was raging, there were barely fifty metres between us and the demarcation lines, but the glass of the shop never shattered. There were bombs and shells and yet the shop was never destroyed the way it was on August 4th. This was like nothing we had seen before. No one came to check on me after, not one official.'

Siham visited at least five hospitals on the evening of the blast before she was taken care of.

'At 3.30 a.m. they stitched me and told me to go home. They could not keep me as there were no beds available. I cried a lot.'

She started crying.

'Where would I go? Which house? I had no house left, I go on the street?

'I went back to the shop. Some men gave me a plastic chair to sit on and another to lean on. I sat in front of the shop to protect it from looting. They put a tissue box under my leg and one under my arm as support. I had stitches everywhere.

'I needed a cortisone injection and could not find any. I had twenty-four hours to find one. I also needed antibiotics and there was none. Then someone found a bottle in the south, in the city of Saida, and brought it for me.'

Since the onset of the crisis in 2019 and because of the Lebanese currency devaluation and the shortage of dollars, the imports of medicine, which became more expensive, slowed down. A lot of drugs disappeared from pharmacies' shelves starting in the summer of 2020, including medicine for chronic illnesses, as people and importers hoarded them. Even baby milk dried up.

My daughter came down with a nasty cold in the summer of 2021, exactly a year after the explosion. I needed antibiotics for her cough and spent a whole day looking for some, hopping from one pharmacy to another, before my friend gave me a bottle she had at home. It was surreal to be in a country that once boasted it imported everything, including the latest luxury cars and designer bags, but was now short of the most basic medicines.

In November 2021 the government partially lifted medicine subsidies, inflating some drug prices to new highs without offering any cash assistance to the most vulnerable, like Siham.

'I used to pay 13,000 LBP for my diabetic medicine. Now it is no longer subsidized, I pay 350,000 LBP, that is about 11 dollars at the new devalued rate.

'I had diarrhoea once, just diarrhoea, and I could not find anything to cure it. I stayed for three days with diarrhoea, no medicine, having to sit here. There was no power, so I would go up and down the stairs to the toilet despite my injury. It was hell. We live in hell. When I finally found the medicine, I felt like I found a treasure, imagine, a diarrhoea medicine. But guess how much it was? Ten times more.'

I buy Siham at least four different types of drugs and send them to her from Paris whenever I can. As of 2020 many Lebanese expats started sending medicine to their families and friends back home. Private initiatives were organized around the world to send batches of medicine through travellers to the country. The Lebanese no longer travelled home bearing gifts but luggage full of drugs and baby milk.

Whenever Siham calls me in Paris asking for medicine, she apologizes.

'I swear I have no choice but I cannot find this medicine here. I have to beg people all the time. I beg friends, I beg pharmacists. I have no choice.'

Every time I send her the drugs, she calls me crying.

'God bless you, I am sorry I am such a burden.'

Siham is among 80 per cent of Lebanon's elderly who have no retirement funds or healthcare coverage, according to the International Labour Organization. They grow old without any social protection, relying on family help when possible or lifetime savings. The state doesn't provide them with any support. Even governmental hospitals have stopped taking them in. My mother runs a retirement home in my home town in the north of Lebanon that my grandfather had founded. It welcomes the most vulnerable elderly, offering them a home. I grew up witnessing first-hand the hardship of these men and women, who end their lives with almost no safety nets. Because of the economic crisis, centres for the elderly, all or most of them privately owned or running on donations, struggled to stay afloat, find private funding and medicine, and pay their personnel. At the same time, they were under mounting pressure to take people in, as more and more families could no longer afford to take care of their elderly relatives.

'We are not very poor, but our money was stolen by the bank. Everything my husband and I had saved for our retirement is now gone. It does not exist,' Siham said.

'After the shop was destroyed [in the blast], the bank only gave me 200 dollars from my savings but in Lebanese pounds and at a devalued rate. It was the equivalent of 533 dollars before the crisis. It was not enough for me to fix the shop and the house. With the help of individuals, I fixed the bare minimum in the house and shop. At night I sit and cry and thank God for his grace. If it weren't for these people, I don't know what we would do.'

A UN report in April 2022 accused Lebanon's central bank and the country's banking sector of 'human rights violations . . . including the unnecessary immiseration of the population that have resulted from this man-made crisis'.

Both Lebanon's central bank and its commercial bank are responsible for overseeing the country's financial collapse.

Starting in 2016, in order to keep the Lebanese pound pegged to the dollar as well as lend the government money, Salameh engineered a Ponzi scheme. It offered commercial banks very high interest rates in return for their deposits in US dollars. The central bank used the deposits to provide loans to the government and preserve the dollar peg. Banks, on the other hand, to keep their USD reserves in check and attract further USD inflows, offered depositors very high interest rates, as much as 20 per cent in some banks. The scheme allowed foreign reserves to stock up again, but banks' liabilities also grew, as did the government's debt. Then in 2019 the scheme was exposed. People's savings and deposits had been depleted by the banks. As people rushed to withdraw their money, they discovered it was now mostly ink on paper. The banks imposed informal capital controls, allowing depositors to withdraw only a limited amount of cash in dollars and halting transfers abroad.

'Look at the shop, it's empty, I can't buy much anymore. Today I bought five boxes of juice, five water boxes. I spend most of the money I make in the shop to pay for the generator. They don't give us power, we need to pay for a private generator, generators need diesel fuel, and now you can't find fuel anymore or it's expensive. This month I paid 15,000,000 LBP [$500] just for the generator fees. If it weren't for the help of some people, I could not pay that.'

Five hundred dollars' worth of generator power for one month provided by a private generator. This is insane. My husband tells me he pays even more on our apartment in Lebanon to keep the power and air conditioning on through the summer. 88 per cent of the income of the poorest families in the country were spent on generators' bills in 2023, according to a Human Rights Watch report. The state's failure to fix Lebanon's electricity infrastructure problem since the end of the war, coupled with corrupt deals to acquire fuel, created a parallel market filled by a mafia of private generator operators. Generator owners, protected by powerful political groups, sold privatized power to households at inflated prices. We always paid two power bills, one for the state, one for the generator.

In 2021, Lebanon witnessed a severe shortage of diesel which further exacerbated its decades-long power cuts. The central bank, after running out of dollars, started lifting fuel subsidies. Oil importers could no longer afford to buy the same quantities and so petrol stations started rationing their supply. The shortage was also caused by hoarding. Private businesses and individuals started selling the fuel at a higher price on the black market, smuggling it to Syria where the profit margin is higher. People queued for hours to get fuel at petrol stations. Some even slept in their cars overnight. Clashes erupted, with a few incidents of civilians, furious and desperate, pointing guns at each other in fuel queues.

Blackouts were more recurrent than ever. Since 2020, Beirut has been literally a city of darkness. Most traffic lights don't work, so you drive in virtual obscurity at night. And it is ironic, because you could be driving in darkness to go for a drink on a fully lit rooftop bar where people are dancing – but around you everything else is black.

'I work all day and make five or six dollars. I am an old woman but I sit here from six a.m. to one a.m. for five dollars a day. How can I afford anything?'

Siham sobbed like a baby. It broke my heart to see her like that. She shouldn't be sitting here, working so long. Women of her age should be thinking of retiring by now.

Two years after the explosion, she was still struggling to keep her business afloat and had not received any form of state assistance. She applied for a grant. The grant would be given to her by the World Bank through a public institution linked to the central bank, the same central bank that had robbed Siham of her savings. When I checked on her again a year later, she told me she got nothing.

'We were doing really well during the civil war. We made money, we used to save them in the bank, we could withdraw money whenever we want to. Now it's just ink on paper.'

The Lebanese have been locked out of their dollar deposits since 2019, myself and my husband included. We just happen to be lucky enough with our careers to be able to start anew and save again. But most people are not that lucky. They cannot retrieve their lifetime savings, not even to rebuild their homes which were destroyed by the same criminal negligence and incompetence that has led to the financial crisis. Many are finding themselves in desperate situations trying to pay for crucial needs and expenses. When and how the Lebanese will get their money back, if ever, is a question I cannot answer. More than $100 billion are estimated to be trapped in Lebanese banks who by early 2023 had still not announced their bankruptcy. Banks still owed an estimated $93.6 billion to depositors in December 2022. And yet, these banks had still not announced their bankruptcy. Some depositors have resorted to courts to retrieve their savings, but they remain individual cases and the judiciary is incapable of holding those responsible to account or giving everyone's money back.

The Central Bank governor on the other hand has been the subject of a local and an international probe. He was being investigated in 2023 by at least five European countries for embezzlement, money laundering, and illicit enrichment. The man who was at the helm of Lebanon's financial policies, who was named the best central bank governor in the Arab world by Euromoney, and received several other international awards, had allegedly amassed a fortune outside of by moving and laundering hundreds of millions of dollars of public funds through offshore companies. The investigation also included his brother and a close associate. As this book was ready to be published, France issued an arrest warrant against Salameh who failed to show up to a questioning session in Paris. Salameh is now a fugitive.

In Lebanon, the state also filed a lawsuit against the Central Bank chief but the capacity of the local judiciary to deliver justice remained in question as Salameh was still supported by a majority of the politicians. He was the banker of the establishment and many would go to great lengths to protect him. Just like in the probe of the Beirut explosion, Lebanese people doubted any of these investigations would bring them justice or return their deposits.

Desperation has led some depositors to resort to force. In August 2022 an armed man held a bank hostage for many hours in a distressed attempt to retrieve money from his account and pay for his father's hospital bill. The stand-off ended with the man getting about $30,000 out of the $210,000 he had in the bank. He was arrested and then released without charges. Many would later attempt to do the same in various banks and regions in a desperate attempt to take out their money. One of them was a woman who also had to pay for her sister's cancer treatment. In September

2022, Sally Hafez held up a bank in Beirut at gunpoint to cash in her savings. The gun she had was only a toy and Hafez, who later turned herself in and then was released on bail, cashed in $13,000 from her account. Thanks to what she did, her sister is now getting treatment in Turkey. 'We are in the country of mafias. If you are not a wolf, the wolves will eat you,' she told Reuters.

'My husband cries day and night,' Siham told me. 'He saved money all his life. We were doing well, we were middle class. He used to tell me let's not travel, let's not spend, we will use them to retire. He was lured by the bank interest rates. The bank convinced him to save and get interest. Look at us now. I wish we spent them and enjoyed our lives. All we did was work and they took it all away.'

Siham sobbed. A young woman walked into her shop as we spoke. She wanted to buy cigarettes. Siham wiped her tears, told her to pay later. 'I love you,' replied the woman. 'Me too, me too,' said Siham.

The power went off in the shop. Siham stood up to switch the power outlet, so the generator was on.

'We have thirty minutes of state power per day, that's it. You see why I have to pay for the generator to get additional hours otherwise all of my produce goes to waste. The minute the state grid is on, I rush to my apartment to bathe my husband and feed him. I don't use the private generator at home as much as I do here, I cannot afford it. So, I am often dependent on the state electricity and that is almost nonexistent.'

When I came to Lebanon in 2022, fuel was no longer in short supply, just very expensive since it was no longer subsidized. Many were rationing the use of private generators and so power cuts were still a problem. Yet, another basic item had temporarily vanished: bread or what the Lebanese call 'rabta', the bundle of Arabic bread that is a staple food item on every household's table. Tens of people queued in front of bakeries for bread that summer. Lebanon's wheat largely depends on imports from Ukraine and Russia, which were affected by the war in Ukraine. Beirut port's silos, damaged by the blast, could no longer store any wheat. Bakeries claimed they had suffered from limited quantities of

subsidized wheat and could no longer keep up with the demand
for bread, which was already getting more expensive after the local
currency crashed.

But what I found striking was that, while bread was in short
supply, croissants, biscuits, French bread, and other wheat-based
items were plentiful. Bakeries were actually using the subsidized
and limited quantities of wheat to make and sell more profitable
goods instead. And just like with fuel, bread and flour were also
being smuggled into Syria on the black market.

With little or no governmental control, some Lebanese,
unfortunately, were orchestrating shortages to feed their greed and
increase their profits at the expense of others' pain.

'I don't have bread this week to sell or to eat. It's been five days.
Not a loaf. The minister says on TV there is enough flour, the
bakeries say they don't have bread. Go figure.'

Customers came in and asked for bread, but Siham had to turn
them away, empty handed. We paused a lot during our interview.
She was busy at work with other things and I didn't want to be an
obstacle, as this was her 'bread and butter'.

'I have nothing against him personally, I am talking as a citizen
suffering. I have no power, I can't buy medicine, I can't find bread.
I have to work day and night. Honestly, I am tired, I am very
tired. I have to provide for two families. I have no children. No
pension funds. The explosion took half of my body from me. I am
very tired. I see dirt in the toilet and I can't even kneel to clean it.
We can't be humiliated more than that. Two years now, every day
is worse. Is it possible to live like that? What are they doing? If
they can't do anything why are they still in power? Sitting on their
chairs and getting paid from our money? They stole our money, let
them go. "Fuck the old man. Let him go home,"' Siham told me,
referring to the then Lebanese president, Michel Aoun.

8

Nowhere Safe

GHOFRAN

'If I chose my life, it wouldn't look like this.'

Nine out of ten Syrian refugees in Lebanon live in extreme poverty, according to the United Nations. They are mostly families that fled the conflict in Syria starting in 2011, settling in neighbouring Lebanon, with the hope of finding safety and making ends meet. Instead, and during the span of more than ten years, Lebanon's successive governments have marginalized and secluded them, always under the pretext of preventing their permanent settlement in the country.

From the onset of the Syrian crisis, Lebanese authorities decided to have a 'no policy' on refugees, refusing to organize them into formal camps, like in Jordan or Turkey, allowing thousands of informal tented settlements to mushroom around the country without the most basic services and infrastructure. There were no sewage systems, no proper waste collection, no clean water. United Nations organizations, including UNHCR, where I worked for four years, tried their best to improve camp conditions, but they were still pockets of misery scattered around the country. Those who did not live in camps lived in unfinished buildings or shops and garages, often paying a hefty rent to Lebanese landlords in return for an undignified living.

Syrians, just like Palestinian refugees who settled in Lebanon many decades before, were also banned from working and taking on jobs and were pushed into the black market, working informally in precarious conditions and relying on international aid whenever possible.

I covered the Syrian refugee crisis in Lebanon from its beginning in the spring of 2011. I co-authored one of the earliest stories about the first families crossing into the north of Lebanon in April of that year. Protests were gaining momentum around Syria and were met with violence by the Assad regime. Coverage of the Syrian refugee crisis would form a large part of my career as a journalist.

Today, it is estimated that around a million Syrian refugees still live in Lebanon. They came to the country in waves, some early on and others later in the conflict, like Ghofran, who fled Syria with her mother and siblings in 2017. She was only 16. The Syrian war was into its sixth year and Islamic State had taken over her town.

'We had difficulties finding bread, there were no job opportunities, there were no schools. Daesh made us wear the niqab. Girls could not get an education, they gave us Sharia books to study. You can't really leave your house, and if they like you, they will take you. If a fighter likes a woman, she becomes his wife the next day. My mother was so worried. I have two younger sisters and three brothers. My father had died three years before. We came here. I got married. I was sixteen. I married my cousin.'

Early marriage is common among Syrian refugees, especially those coming from rural areas. Girls rarely finish their education or have a career. They are looked upon as a financial burden by their parents. Ghofran tells me her mother rushed to get her married, almost as if ridding herself of a burden. When I visited her in 2021, Ghofran was home alone with three children, all under three.

'I never thought of getting married. I wanted to finish school and become a pharmacist. It was my dream.'

She paused and smiled timidly. It felt like that was still her dream.

Ghofran said many of her childhood friends were now in Germany, continuing their education, and she envied them.

I covered refugees for more than seven years. Many of those I met in Lebanon were eyeing a future in the West, because of the difficult conditions in Lebanon. But only a minority made it abroad through legal channels. It was an extremely difficult, long, and selective process, leaving Syrians with the only option of braving the Mediterranean, often dying during their journey to Europe. Security agencies in Lebanon foiled these perilous journeys from the northern coast of the country almost every week. Now with the crisis, many Lebanese were also desperately trying to leave the country through illegal channels. More and more people were boarding small and unsafe boats from the northern city of Tripoli hoping to get to Cyprus. In September 2022, almost 100 people perished drowning off the Syrian coast while attempting the dangerous crossing. They were Lebanese, Palestinian, and Syrian.

'It's better than the suffering here. When I talk to my friends on the phone, I sometimes cry. When they ask me how I am doing, I say I am fine, I lie. They are studying, doing well. I am married, responsible for three children. My husband and I, we fight a lot; our situation is difficult. Sometimes we can't afford to pay rent. I am bearing a burden that is too heavy for someone my age. We were okay when we first got married but now our financial situation is very dire.'

Ghofran's voice broke. Her children were young and draining her. She was in distress.

'I sometimes tell my husband I want to leave him and take the kids. He goes on the balcony and cries. He breaks my heart. He tells me he can't work, he is helpless.'

The onset of the 2019 crisis made Syrian refugees in Lebanon even more vulnerable. The country's economic crash coincided with the drying up of international assistance and funding for refugees in the region, leaving many of them without any safety net.

The Beirut blast came on top of their protracted agony. Ghofran's husband injured his leg during the explosion. He could not work after that.

'I tried to work. I worked in an apparel shop, but the owner of the shop tried to touch me, it didn't feel right. He wanted to pay me for sex. I left after three days. I never told my husband why. He asked me why I left, I told him I couldn't manage being away from the kids. Imagine, my husband couldn't work, someone had to feed the children. And this is what happened.'

She was tearing up. Two of her children were on her lap. The sight of a helpless mother is heart-wrenching.

'Sometimes we don't eat, so the kids can eat. We cannot even afford bread. The owner of the house here wanted to kick us out because we had not paid the rent in six months. I sold the washing machine, the fridge, the oven, I also sold some furniture. No one is helping us. Sometimes I sit and cry. I ask God to kill me. I would rather be dead than see my children deprived of the things they deserve as children. I sit and cry when I see them looking at candies or juice that I cannot buy. The other day I bought a juice bottle, and now every time they ask for juice, I put water in it and give it to them.'

Ghofran sobbed. I asked her to pause. I briefly played with the children before she picked up her story again.

'Covid was difficult, my husband was not working anymore, things got worse, but eventually he went back to work until the blast. The blast ruined us. My newborn daughter was crying the other day. My neighbour found out I had no milk or diapers anymore so she gave me some. You have no idea how happy I was.'

Like many Syrian refugees in Lebanon, Ghofran couldn't return to Syria yet. Her husband was wanted in the army, and their home had been completely destroyed during the conflict.

When I last spoke to her in 2022, Lebanon's government had announced a plan to deport 15,000 refugees per month back to Syria, which it deemed to be safe. It accused the international community of not helping their return. In reality, Syria was still dangerous.

International rights organizations had reported on arbitrary detentions and abuse of returnees. Ghofran's husband would have immediately been arrested by the Syrian regime if he returned.

'Sometimes Lebanese people tell us you Syrians you are the reason behind this crisis, you ruined the country. I feel like people are disgusted by us, by our children, they tell us you only make babies, you don't care about their future. Sometimes I immediately cry. I can't wait till I am back to Syria. It hurts me a lot. Imagine I told you now, you are not welcome in my house. It will hurt you a lot. But I don't think I can go back.'

Racism against Syrian refugees is common in Lebanon. It feeds on a history of animosity with the Syrian regime, which took part in Lebanon's civil war and later occupied the country. But it is also the result of a populist rhetoric fed by political parties, especially Christian parties on the far right. Politicians have been using the refugees as a scapegoat to distract Lebanese people from the failure of the country's leaders.

The Syrian refugee crisis certainly added a burden on Lebanon, especially at a time when the economy was slowing down in 2011. The country's infrastructure was already frail. Lebanese host communities had to share the poor infrastructure and the shortage of resources, including electrical power and water, with large numbers of refugees. Lebanon has the highest refugee per capita ratio in the world. There is no doubt that the massive influx of Syrians following the war in their country added a huge pressure on the country's economy. But the refugees can't be held responsible for the country's economic collapse. Lebanon even benefited from their presence. For years, it has received foreign aid for hosting more than a million Syrian refugees. Since 2015, the country has received $10.2 billion in aid, targeting not only Syrians but also the poorest Lebanese. UN agencies rehabilitated public hospitals and schools, built new infrastructure, and supported vulnerable Lebanese communities that were hosting refugees. But the Lebanese state, accused of exploiting foreign aid on numerous occasions, continued to blame Syrians for taking jobs from Lebanese people and causing the economic crisis, when in reality it had simply failed to govern the country and manage the influx of refugees. Amid the economic crisis, hate speech and racist tirades only exacerbated. The Lebanese blamed Syrians for their woes. In the summer of 2022, as bread became scarce in Lebanon, the UN reported an increase in violence towards Syrians, with refugees being discriminated against in bakeries and even beaten up for trying to buy bread.

It was almost time for me to leave Ghofran, as her husband was arriving home from work and she had asked me not to be here when he came. I asked her if she had any dreams for the future. I was hoping she would tell me she still wanted to be a pharmacist.

'I have no dreams, I just want my children and husband to be happy. I am completely destroyed on the inside. I don't feel what other women feel. I look around me, I see beautiful women, dressed up, with a hairdo, going out with their kids and spouses, God bless them, I wish I could be like that. We don't go anywhere because we can't afford it. I just came back from the grocery shop, I was buying zucchini for dinner. My daughter wanted bananas, but I couldn't afford them. She cried.

'I didn't choose my life, it was my destiny. My parents, my husband, me being here, I didn't choose it. If I chose my life, it wouldn't look like this.'

Also, Ghofran did not choose to become a refugee. No one would choose that.

FATME KINNO

'Sometimes I say I wish I stayed in Syria.'

Ghofran was not the only female Syrian refugee I met while working on this book.

I came across Fatme's story after her daughter was photographed by my former Associated Press colleague in the minutes following the blast. The picture made the front page of most major international media outlets. It's a gory shot of a young woman whose face is covered in blood and who is being carried on the back of a man. It was her daughter Huda, who is still alive today.

But on 4 August 2020, Fatme lost her other daughter, Sidra. She also lost her ability to move and any sense of safety.

She fled the war in Syria shortly after the onset of the conflict there in 2011, only to get caught up in the violence of the Beirut blast. Forty-three Syrians were killed that day, the largest foreign group among the victims.

'We left Syria because of the bombs and the air strikes. We escaped the terror. I saw people get killed. It was terror. I had six kids when I arrived to Lebanon: Mahmoud, Aya, Hassan, Otayba, Sidra, Huda, and then Ahmad was born here. Now I have six children (again).'

In Lebanon they lived in a small room on the ground floor of a building facing the Beirut port, where Fatme's husband worked as a janitor. The children didn't go to school. This remains the case for many refugee children in Lebanon whose parents no longer enrolled them in school after fleeing Syria. Some said they couldn't afford the bus fees to send their children to public schools where free afternoon classes were organized for refugees. Others wanted their children to work to help them make ends meet.

Fatme's eldest daughters Sidra and Huda, aged 16 and 11 respectively, stayed home and helped their mother with the house chores. On the afternoon of 4 August, Sidra made tea for her family – but they never had time to drink it.

'I remember Sidra screaming, I remember that I flew away. I don't even remember hitting the ground. When I woke up my hips were broken, my legs and back were injured. There was dust everywhere. I looked around searching for Huda and Sidra. I saw them laying down close to each other. I saw that my husband hurt his head. It was like an earthquake, indescribable. Glass, wood, trees everything broken. Huda woke up after a while, she kept on crying. Sidra didn't move, I knew she passed away. I looked at her but I couldn't touch her.'

I asked her why.

'I don't know, maybe from the shock, I couldn't touch her. I wanted to touch her legs, they were close to me, I couldn't. One of my sons ran to me saying: Mom, Sidra is dead, Sidra is dead. I nodded as if I knew. My son-in-law used to work nearby, he came to check up on us. I told him Sidra died. He went inside with Otayba, my son, to carry her out. They also carried Huda and put her next to me. She was in pain. She leaned her head on my legs, and I saw that she was in pain. But I was also injured, I couldn't handle the weight of her head on me. I asked her to remove it. Later on, her uncle Mustapha carried her out. That is the famous photo that everyone saw. Abou Mahmoud, my husband, was put on a wooden piece and carried out. Sidra was dead. She stayed in the hospital. Huda had broken bones, she needed an operation.'

Fatme and I were not sitting alone having this conversation. Huda, whose photo became famous, and who survived that day unlike her sister, was sitting listening in silence. I wondered how traumatized she must have been. I wanted to ask her questions but I was hesitant. I was not sure I knew how to deal with a traumatized child.

'We were scared, we were traumatized from the war in Syria, we were scared but we didn't expect something this big to happen. I don't know how to describe it. It destroyed all of Beirut.'

The wounds were still visible on Fatme's legs. I asked her if she was in pain.

'I can't survive without painkillers. I take painkillers for my back, I can't wake up in the morning without them. But the problem is that they are hard to find now. I can't properly walk on my leg. I can't walk for a long distance, I only walk to the bathroom. But Alhamdulillah.'

Alhamdulillah means 'Thank God'.

'It was a difficult year, life became difficult, and it has no meaning. I know that I have six other kids but everyone is different, every child has a special place. I left Syria to protect them. In a few seconds I lost her, for nothing, because of negligence. Our life was ruined, our life turned upside down. In the house, half of us are disabled. Alhamdulillah we can walk but we can't work anymore. Alhamdulillah. Sometimes I say I wish I stayed in Syria, but the situation in Syria is bad as well. There's no fuel or bread there. The war is still happening.'

Fatme and her family have not been back to Beirut since the blast. After the explosion, they moved in with their son in the mountains outside the city, before settling in the south where they are now.

'We couldn't live in Beirut anymore. The children and I couldn't live in Beirut anymore. I feel like it's a city in ruins. We stayed with my son, but then he got fired from his work because he missed a few days when he had to check up on us in the hospitals. They told him "you're skipping work" and fired him. And he was working informally, so you can imagine. He used to work tirelessly sometimes until 11 p.m. The employers didn't sympathize with his situation, they fired him. He couldn't pay rent anymore and so we moved to this place. Our cousins helped us move here. They work here as janitors and live with their families, so now we live here. Here it's better, we can easily buy groceries or anything we need nearby. Alhamdulillah.'

I ask her why she keeps saying 'Alhamdulillah'. What is there to thank God for?

'Alhamdulillah in every state. In good and bad times. I'm a believer, Alhamdulillah. I don't ask for anything. I think it is God's will that she died. I can't talk to God and ask him why? I hope we all go to heaven and meet Sidra there.'

She sobbed. I reached out to hold her hand.

'Sometimes I try to stay strong for my family. Other days, I look for her stuff, her clothes, I put them on the ground and I smell them. She was 16 years old. She was calm, sensitive and caring. She used to help me in the house, she learned how to cook, clean and do the dishes.'

I asked Fatme about Huda. How was she doing? Was she still not going to school?

'We finally enrolled her. She is happy. It helps her. But she has a lot to catch up on. She is twelve now and she is in class with seven year olds. But she is good.

'She used to sleep with her sister in the same bed. They were close. Few days ago, I slept next to Huda. In the middle of the night, she held my hand screaming: "Sidra, Sidra come closer . . ." I woke her up saying "Huda, are you okay?"'

Fatme was still crying. I felt terrible for her, but also for Huda who had to listen to this conversation and see her mother in this state.

Huda finally spoke.

'Is it possible that an explosion will happen here? In this area next to us? Is it possible that we die?'

She had caught me by surprise. I was shaken by her question. So poignant, so significant. My immediate response was to tell her it wouldn't happen. I told her she would be okay. But in reality she was not safe anywhere.

PART THREE

The Impossible Quest for Justice

Even the judiciary in Lebanon has collapsed. Caught between an economic crisis and political interference, the system cannot deliver justice. And without that justice, the country has no future. Lebanon's prevalent culture of impunity prevents it from moving forward.

Many of the women in this book are fighting for justice today for what they lost on 4 August 2020, during the economic crisis and Lebanon's endless wars. But their quest for justice goes beyond that, their loss as women in Lebanon transcends these adversities. They are victims of a system that considers them second-class citizens, that has discriminated against them and abused them throughout recent history. Lebanon has a reputation of being the most liberal country of all the Arab nations, including when it comes to women's rights. Lebanese women gained the right to vote in 1953. Women's literacy rate is among the highest in the region. The country boasts some of the most vibrant feminist movements in the Arab world. But in reality women still face discrimination, legal, institutional and cultural hurdles that prevent them from progressing on the path to equality with men. The economic crisis and the Beirut blast have heightened Lebanese women's vulnerability.

9

Second-Class Citizen

LILIANE CHAITO

*'She was still unconscious when they took her
newborn son away from her.'*

Liliane was one of two women in this book who couldn't get to tell
their own story because they were silenced by the Beirut blast.

The 28-year-old Lebanese mother was also silenced by Lebanon's
patriarchy and discriminatory religious laws.

Liliane woke up from a coma, after sustaining severe head
injuries in the explosion, only to find out that her husband had
taken her newborn son away from her.

She was still in a hospital bed and could speak for herself.
Although she was conscious, understood what she was told and
reacted, she needed proper rehabilitation and speech therapy to
talk again.

I met with her sister Nasma in the summer of 2022 to hear
about her story. Liliane's family had a pending custody battle over
her son Ali with her husband who lives in the Ivory Coast. Ali
was being cared for by his paternal grandparents in Lebanon. They
were refusing to bring him to see his mother or spend time with
her family.

Both Liliane and her husband are Shiite Muslims and their personal-status matters are regulated by the Jaafari Shiite court. The Jaafari court is by far the worst when it comes to women. It grants men complete custody over their sons as soon as they are two and over their daughters as soon as they are seven.

'It was about five days after the explosion. She was still unconscious when they took her newborn son away from her,' Nasma told me.

'Ali was a month and a half only, my mother was taking care of him, helping Liliane because her husband was in Abidjan. Liliane had come to Lebanon that summer to give birth. After the explosion, my mother kept Ali with her. She was staying at Liliane's home but eventually wanted to return to her apartment where she was more comfortable. She called Hassan, Liliane's husband, to ask him if it was okay. He acquiesced. He didn't travel to come and see her and his son, after she was injured. I am not sure why.

'Shortly after he told my mother that she could keep Ali, Liliane's mother-in-law showed up and threatened my mother. She snatched him away. She told my mother that the kid is her grandson, his father was alive but his mother was dead. My mother went crazy, started crying. That was the last time we would really have him with us.'

Liliane was still in a coma but not dead. She eventually started regaining consciousness after 17 days, according to Nasma. Her sister was not very aware at first, but with time she improved.

'Her husband only visited her 25 days later. He didn't bring Ali with him. He acted like a complete stranger. Even a stranger might have cried. He was maybe shocked. I don't know. But he barely stayed with her. He left back to Abidjan a few days later. In retrospect now, I think of it this way: he married a doll, when it became useless, he just threw it away. That's what it looks like.'

Liliane's family kept begging her in-laws to bring Ali to her. They refused, often using health reasons. They asked them to at least let her see her baby son in a video call. They still resisted. Time passed and Liliane became more conscious but also more depressed. She needed her son but was being denied access to him.

'Her in-laws started making up stories about us to justify not allowing Ali to spend time with us. Let us say these stories were true. Why deny Liliane, his mother, from seeing him? What is her mistake? Why should Ali live without knowing his mother? She is not dead. She is alive. She just cannot speak.'

It was not until a local journalist made a fuss about Liliane's custody story on social media that the husband agreed to let her see him on video.

'She cried. He was a baby. He was not even one. He didn't know his mother. She looked so helpless.'

A few months later, Liliane's family found out that her husband, through a Jaafari court decision, had been granted power of attorney over her. Liliane could no longer make any decisions of her own or sign any official documents. Her husband was in full control. Such court orders, according to a lawyer I consulted, are taken when a spouse has a mental incapacity, including insanity, delusion or unconsciousness. Liliane didn't suffer from any of these. She had just not regained the power of speech. According to her medical records, she was capable of understanding and reacting.

'Someone from court came to the hospital to ask about her, but he didn't even go in to see her or talk to us. A nurse told us. The guy came to the hospital briefly and left. Her medical file in the court order was signed by an anaesthesiologist. It was absurd. My sister was conscious and understood everything. On what basis he took custody over her life? We went and faced the judge with his lawyer. They said it was just because of the son. Why? We are going to kidnap him? We only asked that his mother sees him. We don't want to see him. Let her see him. Just a regular video call for God's sake.'

Shortly after, an officer from General Security showed up at the hospital, according to Nasma. He informed her that a request for a passport for Liliane's son had been submitted. He had come to check if Liliane was really unconscious and so unable to sign the application, as her husband claimed.

Back in 2014 a law amendment had made it compulsory for both father and mother to sign passport applications for their kids. Originally, only the father needed to sign, as a means of taking children away from their mothers in cases of dispute or divorce. The law amendment was the fruit of years of advocacy on behalf of organizations for women's rights.

'I told the officer to come and see for himself if she was in a coma. They were trying to issue a passport so his father takes him to Abidjan. We couldn't accept that.'

Around the first anniversary of the blast, and also because of media pressure, the Jaafari court issued a decision granting the maternal grandmother the right to have Ali for four hours a day to take him to see his mother. The court also issued a travel ban so his father couldn't take Ali out of the country.

'But they [the husband and his family] didn't care about the decision. They never implemented it. They even appealed. They have money and power. They are backed by both Hezbollah and Amal party. We have no political support from anyone.'

The court case had not moved on since that appeal more than a year ago. Lebanon's judges had been regularly going on strike protesting low salaries and degrading working conditions. During the economic crisis a judge's monthly salary was about 3,700,000 LBP, or about $90. They couldn't afford to fill the tank of their car to go to court, they had no paper or ink at the court because there was no money to buy any. Thousands of judicial files were in limbo due to the economic collapse.

'We asked for Liliane's passport, we want to take her abroad for rehabilitation. Her husband kept saying there is no treatment for her outside. He refused to give us her passport. We are her family. We have every right to seek what is best for her. It has been a year since we are trying to transfer her to a rehab centre abroad. She got accepted in a centre in Turkey. She needs to leave the hospital. There are no proper rehab centres that can help her in Lebanon. He is doing everything so she stays in the hospital. It is as if he wants to try and kill her once again after she survived the first time. The ministry of health won't help her either. What do we do?'

I asked Nasma if she was not aware of any relationship issues between her sister and her husband.

'It was all good. She had just given birth. Imagine that she was buying him a birthday gift at a shop in the Beirut souks when the blast happened.

'He came recently, in the spring, he didn't bring his son. Liliane didn't even want to look at him. She knows what is happening though we tried to lie to her so she doesn't worry. But she knows her son was taken away from her. Every time she sees a baby on TV, she cries. Every time I show her the photo of someone's baby, she cries. I don't even have his recent photos to show her.'

It must be so painful to suffer in silence, I thought to myself.

'A psychiatrist suggested we buy her a baby doll wearing blue because Ali wore blue when he was born. We did and now she won't let the doll go. She started crying and caressing the doll when we first gave it to her. She knows it's a doll. But she clings to it. She utters the word "mama" when she holds it. It breaks my heart. You have no idea how it felt to see her like this with the doll.'

I started tearing up before she did. Her voice broke. We both cried.

'She is a mother. Why are they denying her seeing her son? Where is humanity?'

We paused.

Nasma looked through her phone. She showed me a video of Liliane undergoing speech therapy at the hospital. She was being asked to press coloured Yes and No buttons to answer questions. She could understand what she was being asked to do.

'We are doing what we can with limited capacities. But she cannot stay at the hospital. We are wasting time.'

Liliane needed specialized care. Her family desperately wanted to move her abroad but they had neither her passport nor the financial resources.

Although Liliane's husband has power of attorney over her life, he is not paying for her hospital bills. An organization has taken charge of that while her family pays for the medicine she needs.

'We had deposits in Lebanese pounds, now it's all been used, we have 20,000 dollars in the bank but can't access that. We can't find the medicine here. We pay someone to get them from Turkey and pay him in dollars but it's been a struggle.'

On 1 August 2022, and following a Reuters story about Liliane, the husband finally gave back her passport.

Liliane's in-laws also showed up with her son Ali on the second anniversary of the explosion. Nasma believed it was just a reaction to the pressure of public opinion.

'It was a short visit and more like a fanfare. Everyone was holding phones and filming. It was so uncomfortable for both of them. When she saw him, she started moving her lips, she wanted desperately to talk. She was shaking and crying.'

Following that visit, an agreement was reached with the husband's family to bring Ali back to see his mother every week. But Nasma said they had not seen him since.

Now that Ali has turned two, if the husband were to divorce Liliane, then legally he would be the sole custodian of their son.

'Our problem is we have no political support. They even think we are apostates because we don't support them [Hezbollah]. I don't think they have a religion. I know saying this might hurt me. They will come after me but I am not afraid. Religion, at its core, respects women, they don't. They use religion to justify abuse and discrimination.'

Following a crowd-funding campaign and a large donation from an anonymous person, Liliane was moved to a specialized rehabilitation centre in Turkey at the end of 2022. When I last spoke to them, her family said she was doing better and responding to the treatment but they had not seen or heard from her son Ali since August of that year.

KARLEN KARAM

'I had to have a male custodian. I was not allowed to make any decisions myself because I am a woman.'

Her story was worse than the worst of Greek tragedies. What Karlen lost on 4 August 2020 was both unthinkable and unbearable. I wondered how she woke up every day, how she was still sane, how she carried on. She lost her husband, her brother, and her cousin, all at once. They were in the firefighter brigade that rushed to the port to extinguish the fire.

'Maybe I am still alive because I want to seek justice,' she told me when we met at the brigade's headquarters, a year after the blast.

Karlen had been at the forefront of protests by families of the victims and a vocal voice for justice in the media.

But is that enough? How long can you fight and at what point do you give up? In Lebanon, few have seen justice served, few have been held accountable. What happens if you don't find that justice? Can you ever find peace?

On top of it all, Karlen had to navigate a patriarchal system that considered her a second-degree citizen simply because she is a woman. The system strips you of everything, your individual rights, a dignified living, your right to protection, your right to life.

'I don't know how I am still standing on my own two feet. I am still alive so I can raise my daughters strong but kind. Strong so they can bear living in this country. Imagine this. I had paperwork to do after Charbel [her husband] died, relating to inheritance and compensation. The Church [religious court] obliged me to have a male custodian. I had to have a male custodian. I was not allowed to make any decisions myself because I am a woman. I need another custodian over my children. I also need a court order every time I must cash in reparation money from the state as a widow.'

Karlen is a Maronite Christian, and so once widowed she cannot be the sole custodian over her children, whereas men can be. The Maronite religious court nominates a male custodian on behalf of the deceased spouse. Also, if Karlen needed to cash in reparation money, inherit from her husband, or decide on any financial matters relating to her children, she would not only need a male custodian in each case but also a civil court order allowing her to proceed.

'If it was Charbel who was alive, he would be the only custodian of the children. But because I am a woman, I need someone else. Thank God, I am on good terms with his family and we are close. His father is now the other custodian. The paperwork was too complicated, too slow. I asked the man who was in charge if the same scenario would have applied if my husband had been a widower. He told me, "Honestly mam? No."

'They think I am going to steal the money my children are entitled to? If I put the compensation money in a bank, half needs to be in the name of my first child and half in the name of the other one. And the biggest joke is that it is only 700,000 Lebanese pounds each [$36 when this book was written]. If I need to withdraw that money, then I have to get clearance from the court. Every time, I cash in the money, I need a court order. I need to submit receipts explaining how I used the money. Can you believe it? They don't consider me as their mother. For the court, I am a thief who wants to rob my daughters, that's how the law looks at me as a woman.'

Karlen was 26 and had two daughters. She didn't work and relied on the support of her extended family now that her husband had gone.

'They even take care of the girls because I have no time, I am always on the go, working to achieve justice. I know one day, when they are older, they will understand why I had to be away. The lead prosecutor, Judge Bitar, asked me if I ever had time to see them. I told him my daughter now asks me where her dad is. I tell her he is with Jesus, he is in your heart. But when she is older, what do I tell her? Your father was killed and I don't know who did it? Because we are in Lebanon? Well no. Maybe my husband, brother, and cousin were on duty, they had to extinguish the fire. But the people who were in their homes, in what should be the safest possible place, and still died? Why? We no longer fear for our children when they go out, we fear for them inside our homes.'

Karlen's husband, brother, and cousin had enrolled together at the Beirut firefighters' brigade a few years ago. They commuted together to work every day all the way from Qartaba, a village in the north of Lebanon about two hours from Beirut.

She described them as passionate firefighters, always driven by their mission.

On 4 August 2020 they were all on shift.

'At 6 p.m., I was serving the girls dinner when he [her husband] video-called me. I wish I had kept a copy of that video. He spoke to Angelina [their daughter], she was next to me on her high chair and I was feeding her. He said, "Ango, look at the firefighters, we are going down to extinguish a fire." He made her listen to the sirens. He was very happy, really, he was smiling. Then he said, "Look at your brother, he is driving the truck today, speeding and rushing as usual. We need to catch up with him, there is a fire at the port, call you later."

'Five minutes later, they said on TV there had been an explosion at Beit el Wassat [the official residence of the then prime minister, Saad Hariri]. Everyone was worried at home. I was like, "Don't worry, the boys are at the port, they are safe."'

But they were not and Karlen would soon find out that the explosion was at the port itself. With her family she drove hysterically to Beirut to look for them.

'We were going into morgues, checking in hospital fridges, uncovering dead people's bodies, looking for people in firefighters' uniforms. Then someone told my uncle that my cousin's body might have been found. He went to check. He was so emotional that he believed it was him. He started hugging a dead man's body, and when he turned him over, it turned out it was not.

'We spent the night at the fire station, which had also been destroyed. Whenever their colleagues came in, they would just avoid us, or look at us and start crying. Then this guy comes in and tells me he saw them. I ran toward him and started beating him. What do you mean you saw them? How could you lie? He started crying, telling me he was sorry, but he didn't know what else to say. We prayed all night. Even their truck had vanished.

'A few days later, we were asked to take DNA tests. I did not have the courage to tell my in-laws to do it, they were still expecting him [her husband] to come back home. I took my daughter instead. She was two and a half years old. I told her we were going to the dentist.

'At the beginning I prayed to God for the three of them to come back. Then I asked God to bring one of them back, at least one. Was it possible that I was going to lose the three of them at once?

'But until then, every day, every hour, I was talking with the police. They would send me photos of a hand, or a leg, or sometimes just some flesh that had been found. I saw all of this and still had hope they might be alive. I thought maybe Charbel was in a hospital and lost his memory, or maybe he'd swam away from the shore and reached Cyprus. I had crazy thoughts.'

It was not until 13 August, nine days later, that they were found.

I was speechless. Those days must have felt like hell for Karlen.

'The night of August 11th, I dreamt of him [her husband]. He was in a tuxedo, waiting for me at the entrance of the church where we got married. There were angel statues around him, just like at our wedding. I was in white but not a dress, I was wearing white pants and a shirt. He looked at me upset and told me "Didn't I tell you there was mass on Saturday? Be patient." A few days later, my dream made sense.

'August 17th was their wedding. Yes, a wedding, it was not a funeral. Boula, my cousin, was not even 21. Nano, my brother, was not even 27. They were both single. We didn't want it to be a funeral. Their coffins were met with champagne, music, fireworks, and gunfire. On that day, we only buried my husband's hand. Nano had a bit of his chest and his legs. My cousin had the remains of his stomach and parts of a leg.

'After 40 days, my mother said she felt like parts of them were still down by the port. My father told her she was crazy. The next day, they found more remains. We reopened my husband's coffin, put his body parts inside and then put the remains of my brother and cousin in the same coffin. We couldn't reopen all three.'

Karlen sighed. Her hands were trembling. But she didn't cry. She wanted to portray herself as a strong woman. Or maybe she was forcing herself to, at least that is how I felt. I could hear what sounded like a knot in her throat. I expected her to shed a tear any minute. But it never happened.

'Ever since I was a little girl, I thought of him as the perfect husband. He is my dad's cousin, tall, handsome, and charismatic. He had such a presence. He was dark-skinned but with green eyes.'

She now smiled.

'Before he became a firefighter, he grew his hair. It was long and straight, and he rode a bike. I used to say to everyone, even in front of him, if I found a man like you, I would get married right away.

'One day, when I was at work at General Security, a taxi arrived and delivered some of my clothes. I was confused so I called Charbel. He told me it was the last time he would pick up the phone, that I should get changed, take the taxi, and do what he says. I took the cab. There were red roses inside and a selection of cards. The first one said "I will love you until the last rose dries up", and I realized there was one dry flower in the bouquet. The driver was roaming around and wouldn't tell me where we were headed. He handed me one card after the other. Finally, he dropped me at Saint Charbel's monastery where he gave me the last card. It said, "I am waiting for you at our favourite spot." It was the bench near the statue of the Virgin Mary, but there was nobody there. I looked around and couldn't find him. Then I spotted an engagement ring in the palm of the virgin. I started crying. Charbel was hiding in the oak tree above me, taking a video. Our life was so simple, our pleasures were simple.'

Behind Karlen was a huge drawing of the firefighters. Charbel was a handsome man.

'There is an anger inside of me that is larger than any sadness or longing. I am happy for them, they left us to go to a better place, better than this nauseating life we are living, but I am worried about my kids.

'One night, out of nowhere, before going to bed, Catherina [her second daughter] asked me whether Jesus had a bed. I replied, "No why would he?"

'"Doesn't he sleep?," she asked. When I replied "Not really", she went on, "And where do daddy, Nano and Boula sleep?"

'I told her, "They are never tired and they always have light so they never sleep." But she didn't take that for an answer. She told me she would get Jesus a bed so he could go to sleep and daddy could come and see us. I told her he couldn't and she started crying. It was the first time she'd cried. She woke up the next day, came over, sat on my bed with her arms crossed and told me: "Daddy came over." She had a big smile on her face and told me he said they all love us so much but cannot leave Jesus alone in the dark.'

Karlen paused. She was really forcing herself not to cry. It must have been exhausting for her to talk about her story.

'Nothing brings me peace as much as visiting their graves. I go to the cemetery at night, around 10 or 11 p.m. I used to go every day, now it's every other day. It's the only place where I can say whatever I want. I can't express myself in front of my daughters or my parents, I rarely ever cry in front of anyone. Charbel didn't like it when I cried.

'You know women in Lebanon are not allowed to go to the cemetery during burials, but I did. I asked the priest whether there is anything in our religion that says it's wrong to go to burials, tradition and social mores aside? He said no, so I went. After we were done burying them, I promised them that I will only cry when I am with them. I am at ease at the cemetery. I cry. I talk out loud. I let off steam. I tell them everything. I know I might be talking to myself, but it comforts me. I go at night because there is no one else. People tell me I am crazy, ask me if I am scared. Scared of what? That they are resurrected? I wish. If the dead really woke up at night, then I always would sleep there.

'They took the men of my family. I am the man now. I am the man and the woman. When I must, I am the strongest of men. If we are protesting and there is violence, they tell the women to step aside, but if we do, who will lead this battle? My little brother who is ten? There are no men or women in this fight for justice. Maybe in the law there is still a distinction, but in grief and anger and truth, there is not. I am willing to die for them. They tell me you won't find justice, but we won't sell their blood. I believe that we will find the truth.'

10

Abuse and Racism

MONA MISTO

*'He used to come home at night like a wolf. I would
hide in the attic so he could not find me.'*

An activist I know shared her phone number with me, saved under
the name 'Oum Rawan' ('Rawan's mother') in Arabic. When I
reached out, Mona was warm and friendly. 'Come whenever,
my love,' she said the first time I called her, 'I don't really go out
anyway.'

When I went to see Mona for the first time, I didn't quite know
what to expect. I could imagine she was in a lot of pain after the
explosion, but I had no idea of the extent to which she had suffered
her whole life.

I first visited her in July 2021, just before the first anniversary
of the blast. She lived in a modest apartment in an impoverished
neighbourhood east of Beirut. She welcomed me in black, from
head to toe. Women in Lebanon wear black for many years after
the death of a family member, often because society expects them
to and judges them harshly if they don't. My grandmother wore
black for decades, first for her husband's death and then for her
brother's.

Mona looked extremely worn-out that day. 'I am very tired. I used to be fit. Now, every day, I wake up with a new pain. I can't even put on my clothes on my own. My wrists here, my fingers, all hurt so much. I am surviving on medication.'

Originally from Syria, Mona came to Beirut in 1997 to live with her now ex-husband, who had moved there a few years earlier for work. She gave birth to three children: Rima, Rawan, and Alaa. Mona knew I had come that day to hear the details of what happened to her on 4 August 2020, but she also opened up about deeper wounds. She started telling me about family life with her ex-husband.

'He was an alcoholic. I was the one who took care of them all, provided for them. I was both the man and the woman in the house. I felt alone, throughout. I did everything. When he came home, he wanted to see that the place was clean, and his food was ready.

'You couldn't ask him for a penny. But he was very generous with his friends. He would give them money to buy beer, food, and dope to get high, that's all he cared about. He humiliated me a lot. He humiliated his kids. He kept insisting they drop out of school and get a job. He told me to make them work in shops. He just wanted them to make money so he could drink more. I would work all day and he would take what I made at the end of the day to buy alcohol. Why did I have to put up with that? With that money, I could have bought bread for my children. He would break things in the house: glass, tables. He would scream and howl until the neighbours could hear him. He would tell me I was a whore. He insulted me. I was fine as long as he didn't touch the girls. But he beat them.'

I was surprised by how open Mona was about her story of domestic violence. We had just met after all, and yet she was keen to go into detail. I had come to a home that was broken by a tragedy, lived in by a family that had been through hell.

'One time I had to call in people to help me rescue my daughter whom he'd locked up in a room. He locked her in when he was drunk. You couldn't recognize her when she came out. I couldn't open the door and my daughter was inside screaming helplessly. I ran out of the house and asked for help. When she came out, her dress was shredded, clumps of her hair had been pulled out, blood was running out of her nose and mouth.

'I reported him to the police many times. They would tell me that they couldn't interfere between a father and his children. So, I filed a complaint against him in three police stations, in Borj Hammoud, Ras el Nabaa, and Sin el Fil. They took him away, locked him up in prison for, I don't know, maybe two weeks or two months max. And then they let him go.'

Domestic violence against women is a story I have covered for many years working as a journalist in Lebanon. Women are often trapped in abusive marriages, told by their families and the religious institutions to stick to their spouse and stay silent for the sake of the family. People even find ways to justify the violence, excuses: She was cheating on him, she's not giving him what he wants, she's too strong and outspoken. These women were rarely offered protection by the authorities. I covered cases where, even after the women were killed, their perpetrators managed to evade justice using protection from a politician or bribing a judge. Mona continued:

'He decided to get help once. The rehab centre gave him medication, so he started mixing and taking all the pills together – the morning, the day and the night pills. He would gulp them all down together with a beer and lie unconscious on the floor.

'This period of our lives was horrible. He would bring his friends to the house, lock me in a room, force me to cook for them, to serve them, then he would get so drunk that he peed himself. I would have to clean him up. I didn't resist, afraid of any retaliation in front of the kids. I would do everything he asked so they could sleep peacefully and go to school the next day.'

This last sentence summed up what I had heard from most women survivors of domestic violence in Lebanon, 'I did it for my kids.'

They would bear the mistreatment until their last breath, thinking it protected their children. Mona finally decided otherwise, but it was only after many years of abuse.

'After I filed for divorce, I rented a ground-floor room on my own with the children. One night, he came and kicked the door down. It was a wooden door. I was asleep and heard the loud banging. I looked at the phone, it was 2.30 a.m. I got so scared, and before I even had the time to get out of bed, he broke the door down. It had two shutters. He broke it and then sat down on the floor. He started screaming, telling me this was his place and I had to leave. Then he took a screwdriver and held it up to the neck of my daughter Rima. She was eleven. He always went after her first because she was the eldest and stood up to him.

'I had left a coffee pot on a tray on a table next to my bed. He ordered me to go and get him some. I told him it was empty and cold, but he insisted. I made myself go and get it, to avoid more violence, but as soon as I did, he picked up the cup and tossed it at Rima and then threw the saucer at me. I started screaming, calling on the neighbours for help. They came and took him away.

'That same day, I was brushing my hair and the girls squealed. I asked them if there was anything in my hair. They went silent. I had a bald spot, that big [Mona gestures to show me where] because of the scare he gave me that night. There were days when I would come home and see him sleeping on the pavement of the street next to our apartment. He would be in shorts and tank top, an empty beer bottle next to him. Imagine, seeing your husband lying in the street, people making fun of him. He refused to give me a divorce. The Sunni religious court asked me to reconcile with him, the judge did, many times.'

The second time I visited Mona, she told me that the court had finally granted her the divorce, which was almost impossible. But it still managed to partially blame her for it.

'They wrote on the paper that it was seventy-five per cent his fault but that I was responsible for twenty-five per cent. The clerk at the court told me they had to somehow blame the woman, even if it wasn't true. So, they wrote that I picked the wrong husband and did not do enough to fix the marriage.'

For both Shia and Sunni Muslims, divorce is the absolute inalienable right of the husband but not the wife. That means the man can terminate his marriage unilaterally, without justifying it, and outside a court of law. Women on the other hand have to go to great lengths to justify wanting to end a marriage and are only granted a divorce in exceptional circumstances. Sunni courts also often find the women partially guilty even in cases of abuse and reduce their pecuniary rights. The man is never 100 per cent responsible, there is joint responsibility for the end of the marriage. Women become desperate and sometimes pre-emptively relinquish financial settlements just so their husband sets them free.

'My life was difficult, but after I divorced him and lived with the kids alone, we found some peace, we were able to make ends meet. Rawan was studying and working as a model and as a bartender. She was gorgeous and a lot of advertising companies were after her.'

I had seen Rawan a few times at the bar where she worked, though we'd never spoken, but she was truly gorgeous and very dynamic. Customers later told me that they adored her. She was ambitious and worked hard.

'The morning of August 4th was beautiful, it really was. I woke up with her, made coffee and we went to drink it on the balcony. I can still remember how she was drinking her coffee and scrolling on her phone. I don't know what she was looking at, I was sitting next to her.

'When she wakes up in the morning, the first thing she wants to do is to have coffee with me. If she saw one cup, she would say, "Oh, you are having coffee without me?" So, I would rush to get her cup and we would sit together on this balcony and listen to Fairuz. We would turn YouTube on, and she would ask me, "So, where to today?" We would sit and watch videos about Australia, France, Japan. It was our daily escape together.

'To this day, I put two cups of coffee on a tray. I cannot put just one. I pour one for me and one for her, every day, her cup is always with me.'

Mona went silent for the first time in our conversation.

'If she doesn't see her cup, she will get upset with me and will tell me I am selfish and I have forgotten about her.' She started to cry.

'If I cry for her all my life, it would not be enough. She was getting ready, putting the lunchbox I gave her in her bag, and told me she had to go. I remember asking her, "What is this job? You were off for two days and now you are back on for two? There was coronavirus for two days and now there isn't any?" There was a weird lockdown at that point. Two days on and then two off. She laughed and said, "Yes you see, corona comes for two days and leaves for two."

'I also told her that I wanted to make a plan for her birthday on August 15th. She was going to turn twenty-one. She told me to arrange it on a Saturday and didn't want many people, just us. I told her I'd celebrate her birthday and her brother's at the same time and would bake a cake. She kissed me and left.'

Mona wept. I felt uncomfortable. I was trying to keep a professional and physical boundary between us, but I was now feeling uneasy about her vulnerability.

'Rawan told me she might sleep at her friends in Mar Mikhael that night. I told her not to. She begged. She promised to call me once she got to work. She left at 5:40 p.m. . . . . If only I knew, if I knew, I would have held her by the legs, her clothes, I would have torn my body open, put her in me, just to keep her from going.'

Mona started sobbing hysterically. There was a long pause.

'I was calling Rawan and her sister all the time to no avail. Rima finally picked up and said she was okay, but my calls to Rawan didn't go through. We started running looking for a car to take us to her. Then my brother called from Syria. He told me there had been a huge explosion at the port and started screaming, "Where is your daughter, where is your daughter, go look for her, go look for her."'

Mona told me she needed another break. She left the room for 10 minutes and came back looking calmer.

'I suffer every day. If I look at her sister, I suffer. If I see her brother, I suffer. Rima is alone now, what did she do to deserve that? They were like twins, only a year apart. They did everything together. It was her birthday a month ago, she didn't stop crying. She screams at night, tells me she wants to smash her head, she wants to kill herself, she doesn't want to live without her. How can I tolerate all this? What can I say?'

Rawan's sister was in her room the whole time I was talking to her mother. She never came out. Mona told me her other daughter had stopped going to work, stopped seeing people, and was severely depressed.

'We both saw a doctor and took pills but what can a doctor do? The sounds and images in my head, what I saw, the whole day of August 4th, when they told me she was dead, the screams, none of that ever leaves me. Sometimes I just feel like I want to scream. I want to scream so loud to release that pain inside. There is something in my heart, something that won't get released, and it won't until I am reunited with her.

'They called me the next day, August 5th.'

She paused.

'I don't like to recall that moment. It upsets me so much. Her friend called me, said "We found Rawan." I said "Thank God, Thank God, where? Where?" Then she went on with the next part. I don't know what that did to me. I felt like my heart had stopped. I fell down. I screamed. I threw the phone.

'I need to stop now. I can't. I feel like my heart is being cut into pieces.

'I am sorry. They infuriate me, they tell me I have an angel now, I don't want an angel in the sky, I want her next to me.'

Mona sobbed.

'Two days before, she was standing next to me in the kitchen. She hugged me and cried. She told me, "Mum, please stop working, I am here for you, I will support you, I have a lot of work. I'll pay for rent, for food, don't you worry, anything you want." I told her I cannot sit and do nothing. If I get a job, I'll take it. She went on, "I am never going to leave you mum, I am here for you. I don't want to see you suffer anymore; I like it when you are happy." Where do I get the happiness from now that she's gone? She told me, "I am your support", but she left me alone.

'I go to visit her. I go to see her, but all I see are stones. I miss her. I go. But I suffer more. I keep telling myself she is travelling. I listen to her voice messages. "Hi mum", "I miss you mum." I smile and pray to God that he brings her back to me, that he protects her. My mind cannot grasp where I am, where she is. I gasp every time I remember.

'What happened to us is bigger than any pain anyone can tolerate. They tell me it's been a year. I will feel the same for the rest of my life. I told you how much I've suffered in my life. All the violence, the insults, the glass he broke over our heads. I used to cry, to hurt, but I went on, tidied the house, and put a smile on my face for my kids. I used to pack my worries away in a bag and shove it. I did not complain. I went on.

'He used to come home at night like a wolf. I would hide in the attic so he could not find me. He would look everywhere, he would bark like a dog, bawl, until he would give up and sleep. I took it all on. People would tell me to leave him and leave the kids with him, to go live my life . . . but I wanted my kids to go to school, I wanted them to thrive.

'What hurts me most is that with everything I have been through, I also ended up losing my daughter.

'My God, I was oppressed my whole life. I was never happy with my husband. I didn't have a partner. I was alone with the kids. I didn't live a married life. When I look back at those years, the children are my only solace. He used to think two girls were too much. He mocked me until I had a boy.'

In this part of the world, boys are still considered to be the future breadwinners of the family, and having a boy means continuity and a secure future for the parents. Women are pushed to keep having children until a boy comes. Boys are treated differently to girls. Even in my own extended family, which is less conservative than Mona's, the boys get special treatment, inherit more, and are considered as the heir of the family. Mona tried to defy all that.

'I would tell him I had the most beautiful girls in the world. They had each other. But look at them now, one is gone.

'He came like a stranger to the funeral and then left. The next day he started asking for the reparation money. He is very happy now – the Islamic court ruled that he can get two-thirds of the money and I get one-third. When I feel better, I need to go find the Sheikh to show him the divorce papers, and what he did to me, that he was an alcoholic, a junkie and now a dealer. I am willing to give up that money entirely if it means that he doesn't get a penny of it. Rawan hated him.'

Regardless of religious affiliation, all women in Lebanon face discrimination in inheritance and distribution of marital property after a divorce. For Sunni Muslims like Mona, in the case of the loss of a child, a mother gets only one-third of the inheritance or reparation money and a father is entitled to two-thirds. The second time I went to see Mona, and although the reparation money had not come in yet, she had seen a lawyer based on my recommendation and was trying to get the court to overturn the decision.

And as if this tragedy was not enough, Mona told me that the General Security of Lebanon was not renewing the residency papers of her other daughter, Rima, who had just turned 18. They wanted to deport her to Syria. Rima had lost her sister to an explosion caused by the criminal behaviour and negligence of Lebanese officials. She had been born and raised in Lebanon all her life and had never set foot in Syria. Now she was being told to leave her grieving mother and brother and go to a place where she did not belong. This is the bleak reality of a failed state, where nothing makes sense anymore, where criminals roam free, and the most vulnerable and marginalized pay a hefty price for crimes they did not commit.

Mona started weeping again. This time I decided I'd had enough of watching her break down. I sat next to her and hugged her. Finally, I also cried.

FOZIYA

'I was almost sixteen when I came here . . . They took my passport away.'

Foziya and I walked seven floors up to her apartment as there was no power to take the elevator. The two-bedroom apartment she shared with other migrant women was located on the last floor of a building in the suburbs of Beirut and had only a small window. We were in the middle of July and it was hot as hell. I kept praying for a breeze throughout our time together.

'I was almost sixteen when I came here,' Foziya told me anxiously. 'I wanted to work to support my family. I worked for a family in the suburbs of Beirut.'

I met Foziya through the Anti-Racism Movement, an organization working to defend migrant workers' rights in Lebanon.

Fozi, as she calls herself, came to work in Lebanon in 2007. She was a minor trafficked legally from an agency in her home country of Ethiopia to a recruitment agency in Beirut through what is known as the 'Kafala system', a modern slave-labour sponsorship scheme used in the Arab world to recruit migrant workers.

Fozi did not read her contract before travelling, and once in Lebanon she was made to sign another contract in Arabic, a language which she didn't speak at that time. Little did she know about the labour system that turns domestic workers, mostly from Asian and African countries, into prisoners in their employers' homes.

For almost a decade, I covered the story of migrant domestic workers in Lebanon. Year after year, women working as maids under 'Kafala' suffered exploitation and abuse with no protection from the law. These workers do not fall under the labour system, and their legal residency is directly and exclusively tied to the employer who is their sponsor. They cannot end or change their employment without the sponsor's approval, even in the case of abuse. If the migrant worker leaves her employer without consent, she is considered as an illegal resident and faces detention and deportation.

The result of such a system, in a society that is still largely racist, is forced labour and exploitation for these women with almost no access to legal counselling and support.

The exploitative journey starts upon their arrival at Beirut airport. These migrant workers, who are mostly women, are separated from the rest of the travellers and put in a small room for the General Security agency to process their paperwork. They are then released to meet their employers.

Fozi claimed she had a good sponsor, though that seemed like an exaggeration to me.

'My employers were nice,' she said, then she told me seconds later that she had a friend who used to work standing up for the whole day.

'She was prohibited from sitting down. Madame needed to see her standing up.'

'Madame' is what domestic workers call their women employers in Lebanon. The word felt so condescending to me and echoed the patronizing attitude of many Lebanese households towards these foreign workers.

I asked her if 'Madame' took her passport when she came here. Most employers in Lebanon confiscate the workers' documents upon their arrival, for fear of 'escape'.

'They took my passport away from me. But they didn't really hide it, I knew where it was. She just did not give it to me.'

Foziya either did not understand the severity of having her passport taken from her or was trying to protect herself from criticizing her former employers whom she refused to identify to me. I am not using her last name so as to protect her, as she still lives and works in Lebanon.

I asked her where she slept in the house.

'On the balcony, it was sealed with glass windows. I had a couch bed.'

Migrant domestic workers, estimated at around 250,000 in 2021, live on the margins in Lebanon. Confined to their employers' homes, they lead a lonely life denied of any privacy. Many like Foziya go on living for years in a home without having a proper bedroom or a private space. They rarely get to go out on their own or build ties with their expatriate community. They certainly do not integrate in Lebanon's society.

'Of course, everything was difficult. I was away from my family and even if the house owners were nice, I felt like a stranger.'

She smirked but said no more.

It was very hard to get her to speak openly to me. Foziya was shy but also seemed afraid. She tried throughout our meeting to water down the working conditions she had been subjected to.

When we met in 2021, she had already left her employer 'to make more money'.

'They eventually let me go, they were not willing to pay me more and I needed more money,' she said.

I asked her how much she made with them.

'When I first arrived, my salary was one hundred dollars per month, after two years it became a hundred and fifty dollars. At the end, after eight years, it was two hundred dollars.'

These were the average salaries of a migrant worker employed full-time in a household before Lebanon's economic crisis. A modest sum in return for long hours of work. Foziya worked seven days a week, sometimes from as early as 6 a.m. to as late as 2 a.m. She did not just clean the house, she also took care of the children and cooked.

'I had days off but not regularly. I only had days off after two years of working for them.'

It is very common for Lebanese households not to give a day off to their domestic workers. No one holds them legally accountable for that. I have argued again and again with people I know, including family, over that right and have heard back things like 'we take her out with us, that is enough', 'she will meet someone and fall in love and that is a problem', or things like 'she will start making friends and they will convince her and help her escape' or 'she says she does not need a day off and does not want to go out alone'. Each of these answers was as bad or worse than the last one and there were serious implications of human rights being abused. These women are looked upon as products or machines, owned by their sponsors and denied the right to have a life outside of the home they work in. Legally, they are not allowed to marry or have children in Lebanon.

On top of the tough working conditions and alienation, these women are also subjected to physical and sexual abuse. Fozi says she was not physically abused by her employers, although many other women like her are. I covered tens of cases during my career in Lebanon where domestic workers were either beaten up, molested or raped.

Their suffering is so unbearable that in 2008 a Human Rights Watch report indicated that on average more than one domestic worker was dying each week in Lebanon, mainly from suicide, for example by jumping out of a high building to escape an employer. I reported on many stories of suicide in which the employers always denied wrongdoing and blamed the tragedy on 'mental health' issues. The police never hold the employer accountable or even investigate the death. The migrants' embassies rarely intervene.

It took Lebanon's financial collapse to publicly expose the kafala system. The abuse was no longer silent and happening behind closed doors. As the national currency collapsed and people lost their savings, many employers shifted the economic burden onto these vulnerable women. They stopped paying them, claiming they had no foreign currency. They abandoned them outside consulates and embassies in Beirut. Hundreds of migrant workers camped out on the streets. They had no money, often no passports or tickets to fly back home. Some were able to leave through the support of organizations and embassies, and many still linger in Lebanon today in precarious conditions.

On 4 August 2020 these women, including Foziya, were also victims of the blast at Beirut's port, and they had no safety net or protection.

'That day I don't want to talk about it. I don't want to talk about it with anyone because I want to forget it,' Foziya said.

She looked terrified just in saying those words.

'I was working as a cleaner in a bank in Gemmayzeh. We didn't know what happened. I just said to myself this is the end, I'm going to die now. I fell on the floor and when I woke up, I was surrounded by rubble. I looked up and realized that my hand was broken. I was bleeding. I was stuck under a cupboard, shouting for someone to help me. A man in the room heard me but couldn't see where I was. He saw my hand waving and came to rescue me while stepping on broken computers. I managed to get out of the rubble, my shoes were stuck inside. The man told me to get out and save myself. He said go down and ask for help. I went down and I saw that everyone was injured, everyone was bleeding. People were screaming for help. I looked around, I saw bodies everywhere. I asked a girl to help me, she told me that she needed help as well. We helped each other, we walked looking for an ambulance. We kept walking on the shattered glass, and my legs were hurting me. I couldn't walk anymore. I saw a guy running and stopped him for help. He said he couldn't help me, but he gave me his T-shirt to wrap it on my hand and stop the bleeding. I continued to walk until I met a guy from Sudan. He tried to help me, but he was also busy with himself. I sat down in the middle of the road crying. An Ethiopian woman passed by. I told her, can you please help me, I think I'm dying. I don't have anything with me, not even my ID. If I die no one would recognize me. She didn't leave alone. A guy came to pick her up on a motorcycle and she said to him that she can't leave me alone to die. He took us both on his motorcycle to a hospital. It was full, they couldn't accept anyone anymore. I asked the Ethiopian woman and the guy with the motorcycle to just take me where Ethiopians usually gather in Beirut because I was starting to feel dizzy and will soon pass out. They took me to Sassine's square, they dropped me off where the Ethiopians were standing.'

I asked Foziya why she wanted to go where the Ethiopians usually gathered, instead of to a hospital. It didn't make sense to me.

'Because no one else will help me. At least I will be with my people, they won't leave me. I gave the girl a number she would call if I die. It was my brother's. I told her not to leave me alone because no one would recognize me. They took me to Hotel Dieu hospital, it was full, they did not take me in. The taxi driver left us and said to the girl that I was dying. I can't die on the streets like that. The girl was so scared. She dragged me to the hospital door begging for help. An ambulance arrived, the girl started to scream, some people gathered around me and said I was dying. They put me on a rolling chair and pushed me inside. I insisted on the girl not to leave me alone, not because I didn't want to die but because no one would recognize me if I did.'

This was the third time Foziya had said no one would recognize her. She must have felt so invisible in Lebanon, so insignificant.

'A doctor closed my wounds. My toes were cut off, they stitched them back. My arms were seriously injured, the glass pierced my skin. The Ethiopian girl got a bed for me, it was covered with blood, she cleaned it. I stayed there for three days and on the third day I had an operation on my hand. I kept asking them how much I will pay. I didn't know how much it will cost me. I couldn't believe it when they said to me I don't have to pay. I was so worried about the payment. I thought that I would be trapped in the hospital because I won't be able to pay.'

Foziya did not have to pay her hospital bill that day. She received free care but said she was denied any form of financial support in the days that followed.

'I went to Gemmayzeh to the place where they were giving help for the injured from the explosion. I asked them for help. They saw me suffering as I couldn't walk but they said to me there's no help. I did see people coming in, taking aid, but I was told there's no help. Maybe because I am Ethiopian? Another organization asked me to bring my medical report in order to get help. They took it but never helped me. UNICEF helped me once, covering for one physiotherapy session which was one hundred and twenty dollars. But that is it. I have no support beside my friends.'

Foziya was still recovering from the injuries in her legs when we met. She had not been back to work yet. Her roommates were paying her share of the rent. Organizations like ARM were also supporting her to make ends meet.

When we spoke over the phone a year later, in 2022, Fozi told me she was back to work. This time she was under a new sponsor, who did not employ her directly but only managed and renewed her paperwork in return for exorbitant amounts of money. He was like a fake sponsor, legally responsible for her residency, but who allowed her to freelance in return for part of her salary.

She told me she planned to leave Lebanon but couldn't for now. She could not afford a return ticket. With soaring inflation and a collapsed currency, it had become very hard for migrant workers to save money. Many of them were no longer paid in dollars.

Fozi was not allowed to open a bank account in Lebanon legally because of her status as a domestic worker. In the past, she had sent money to her family. Now, she was barely making ends meet. She also told me that the area she came from in Ethiopia was still rife with conflict and instability.

'I can't go now, but I will one day. There is so much racism here. I'm an Ethiopian woman. Whatever I do or work in, I'll always be seen as a cleaning lady. That's my identity here, even if I stopped doing that for a living. I cannot be more than that to Lebanese people and so I have no future here.'

Despite the financial crisis and the abusive working conditions, migrant women were still coming to Lebanon to work in 2022, although less than before. Some countries like the Philippines have banned their nationals from travelling for work to Arab countries because of the widespread reports of abuse. But not Ethiopia. The trafficking network which starts back in Addis Ababa is lucrative for Ethiopians and Lebanese alike. Ethiopian authorities seem to have turned a deaf ear to the suffering of these women in the Arab world.

I tell Foziya that there were about 20 Ethiopian women aboard a flight I recently took to Beirut from the United Arab Emirates.

'I tell them not to come. I tell them not to come to work in Lebanon. There's a recruitment officer that I saw hitting a girl from Bangladesh. I really cried when I saw her. She went to him asking for help because her employers weren't giving her enough food to eat. He hit her; I saw him hit her. I tell them don't come and work here, especially in people's homes. You live with them, work for them and do everything for them. You won't have a life. They own you.'

This summed up not just Fozi's story, but the story of almost every migrant domestic worker in Lebanon.

11

A Doomed Revolution

Lebanon's collapse coincided with a social awakening and unprecedented mobilization. I would like to think that this awakening is still alive, but I am not so sure anymore. For many, including me, the country's uprising, which started in 2019 with the hopes of becoming a revolution, has transformed, three years on, into a disillusioned dream.

Thursday 17 October 2019 is a date that many Lebanese will always remember. The weeks and months that followed made us believe in Lebanon again. It made us believe in a better future, one in which Lebanon is a nation where we become equal citizens, one where women would have equal rights to men, and politicians would be held accountable. That optimism soon faded.

It was a Thursday night and the government had announced a tax hike including on WhatsApp calls. People, angry and already feeling the burden of deteriorating economic conditions, took to the streets in large numbers in downtown Beirut. Several economic indicators were pointing to a growing crisis, including a mounting pressure on the pegged exchange rate.

At the beginning, I was very sceptical about the protests. I remember watching the protesters gather in a square close to my office and wondering how different it was going to be this time around. This was not the first time Lebanese had mobilized. In the past decade or so there had been various waves of protests that had always dissipated.

In February 2011, encouraged by protests in Tunisia and Egypt, thousands of Lebanese took to the streets protesting the sectarian system. It was the largest civil mobilization since the protests of March 2005 that led to the withdrawal of Syrian troops from Lebanon. But soon the movement was co-opted and sabotaged by the politicians themselves, who endorsed the protesters' demands, claiming they also wanted an end to the sectarian system and calling on their supporters to join the movement.

Then in 2015, Beirut witnessed a wave of protests following a crisis of garbage waste management. Many Lebanese mobilized against the government which, following the shutting down of a landfill south of Beirut, had failed to find a solution to waste management, leaving the country drowning in a sea of waste. I was covering Lebanon for a local TV station and extensively reported on the protests led by a movement called 'You Stink', in reference to the political elite. Demonstrations often turned violent as the police cracked down on demonstrators with tear gas and water cannons. The movement wanted a solution for the waste-management crisis but went beyond that, condemning the political system and demanding political reform.

The garbage crisis represented the epitome of governmental incompetence. Protests lasted a few months but very quickly lost momentum.

Both waves of popular discontent in 2011 and 2015 failed to spark reform to the system or force a change to the country's leadership. In both cases, politicians managed to find ways to demobilize the people on the streets.

The year 2019 felt like a continuation of the awakening and popular discontent that had started in 2015, only this time the participation was unprecedented. The crowds were much larger and more organized. People protested not only in Beirut but in other cities like Tripoli and Nabatiyeh, where affiliation to traditional sectarian parties, including Hezbollah, was dominant. Politicians were named and shamed in public, even chased out of restaurants. They were no longer untouchable.

Seeing this nationwide movement grow, I soon changed my mind.

The Lebanese seemed to be finally breaking their shackles from politicians who had ruled their lives for decades.

I was a correspondent and producer for the Associated Press in Beirut at the time, and I covered the protests. It was a euphoric moment for many, and I felt so lucky to be reporting on a story that was a historical milestone for my country.

On the first days of protests, roads were blocked everywhere with burning tyres. I hitchhiked rides with strangers and walked for miles to get to downtown Beirut where massive crowds had gathered. People came from everywhere across the sectarian divide, both young and old, to decry Lebanon's political establishment. The movement was organized through calls on social media. It had no leadership, no political movements, only citizens angry at those who were leading the country towards its demise.

Sunday 20 October 2019 was probably one of the largest protests in Lebanon's history: a sea of people swarmed into downtown Beirut. Demonstrators waving Lebanese flags called for the government to step down. They were openly chanting against politicians, including the leader of Hezbollah, Sayyed Hassan Nasrallah and his allies. People seemed to have broken the barrier of fear.

Women often led the protests, protecting the crowd with their bodies from baton-yielding security forces, chanting and screaming: 'This is also our revolution.' They have been marginalized over and over again by Lebanon's politicians and the system that they had put in place. Women were out protesting against politicians but also advocating for their rights to be equal citizens, for their sexual freedom, for their right to live.

Lebanon has been led by men for decades, men who fought wars and then turned politicians, men who made fortunes from state resources and then also robbed us of our savings, men who claimed to be leaders but have led our nation to its demise. The women protesters in 2019 were not the first women on the streets, nor the first Lebanese women to advocate for their rights, but we were probably the most visible. For decades, Lebanese women had fought for social and political rights: Warde Boutros, a union activist killed on the streets by police in 1946 while advocating for labour rights; Laure Moghaizel, an attorney who advanced women's rights in Lebanon and the Arab world as early as 1949; Soha Bechara, who took up arms against Israel's occupation of Lebanon and its collaborators in the 1980s; Linda Matar, an activist who dedicated her life to fight discrimination in laws; Wadad Halawani, who has been relentlessly fighting since the 1990s to learn the fate of those who disappeared during the civil war. These women and others like them have shaped our history and continue to do so every day.

As protesters swarmed across the country, banks panicked and imposed a two-week closure citing security concerns. In fact, they were just buying time. The closure would prove detrimental to the sector and the economy. It would hasten a bank run among depositors as soon as the banks reopened, exposing what was revealed as a massive Ponzi scheme orchestrated by the central bank.

The protests continued and the movement's first tangible achievement was the toppling of the government of the prime minister, Saad Hariri. But the one that replaced it, the government of Hassan Diab, was merely a puppet government appointed by the same political leaders. There was growing anger and frustration among protesters who felt duped by the politicians in power.

Soon, the political establishment fought back on the streets. The protest movement was thwarted by a counter-revolution orchestrated by the elite itself. Hezbollah's supporters raided the protests more than once, clashing violently with demonstrators and destroying their tents.

The police cracked down brutally, responding with tear gas and rubber bullets. Many protesters were injured and arrested. A campaign to discredit the protests ensued. Protesters were accused by the political parties, and media outlets affiliated to them, of being manipulated by foreign powers and agents. A baseless conspiracy was put together to weaken the support of the movement and discourage Lebanese from joining the protests in greater numbers. The movement remained largely leaderless.

At the beginning, the lack of leadership was a strategy to protect the movement from any attempts by the political class to attack it and co-opt it. But with time, it proved counterproductive and contributed to weakening the protests.

Early on, divisions started to surface. Old establishment parties like the right-wing Christian Phalangist Party, now rebranded as the Lebanese Social Democratic Party, and the far-right Lebanese Forces Party, both staunch opponents of Hezbollah, claimed a role in the uprising. Meanwhile other groups accused them of being part of the establishment and riding the protest wave for opportunistic reasons.

The main slogan of the protests, 'All of them means all of them', calling on the ruling elite to step down, also divided people. Some groups disagreed with it, saying it diluted the demands of the protesters and weakened its focus. Others wanted the protests to focus mainly on Hezbollah and their weapons, saying they were Lebanon's main problem.

Eventually, the coronavirus pandemic accelerated the fizzling out of the movement. The economic hardship only drained the people. Then finally came the explosion at the Beirut port on 4 August 2020.

The blast breathed a brief new life into the protest movement, sending large angry demonstrations into the streets, with no care for the pandemic. I was also back on the streets covering the explosion and its aftermath. The protest in downtown Beirut on 8 August was probably the most violent one I have ever covered in my career in Lebanon. The police fired massive amounts of rubber bullets and tear gas at the protesters, many of whom had just lost their homes and their loved ones. Police even used live ammunition. Many were injured. The government resigned the same day in the evening. Eight members of parliament resigned as well. But no other political leader or senior official was compelled to quit or apologize for failing to protect Beirut and its people. No one was held accountable.

France, which had played a historic role in Lebanon, was the first foreign country to intervene. President Emmanuel Macron was the first leader to visit Beirut days after the blast. He was warmly greeted on the streets by the Lebanese, who expressed their anger at their leaders. He promised the people that he was on their side. He pledged to urge the elite to push through economic and political reforms, but ultimately he failed to keep any of his promises. Macron seemed to have little leverage and would be late in imposing sanctions on Lebanese politicians, unlike the United States which had started imposing sanctions on Hezbollah politicians and their allies as early as 2019. Some analysts even suggested that Macron provided politicians from the Lebanese establishment with coverage and bought them time. Through his empty promises, he might even have helped to dampen down the popular momentum on the streets.

The protest after the blast was the last such mass gathering. Despite everything they had suffered, the Lebanese chose not to go back onto the streets. Those in power remained in place. For many, including myself, the protests fell short of being a true revolution.

But just as in 2011 and 2015, and like every mass mobilization juncture in Lebanon's history, new groups and narratives surfaced. They were not enough to bring down the political leaders and warlords, but they were also not insignificant.

The movement of 2019 gave rise to new political groups that prepped for parliamentary elections. These groups had participated in the uprising from the outset and now managed to form themselves into actual political movements that would pave the way for a new generation of MPs in 2022. They were non-confessional, transcending sectarian and regional divides, and presented themselves as anti-establishment with the aim of creating a secular Lebanese state. They ran on a platform against Lebanon's sectarian system. They opposed political continuity through family inheritance and want to distance themselves from politicians affiliated to the establishment. They campaigned around social justice, the rule of law, and economic reforms. Some were existing parties that had rebranded themselves and presented a modern vision for Lebanon, but most were newcomers, operating either independently or under the umbrella of larger civic groups.

However, these newbies were far from being a uniform entity and they did not run for parliamentary elections in 2022 as a united consensus. Many competed against each other instead. Few had comprehensive national programs and a clear vision for the many issues that enmeshed Lebanon in the crisis.

Despite these divisions, the 2022 parliamentary elections resulted in a surprising outcome. Thirteen new MPS were elected out of the 128 parliamentarians, which exceeded expectations.

Despite Lebanon's flawed electoral system, which was put in place by the ruling elite to consolidate its power, the results were good. The seats of the new MPs had been taken mainly from long-time establishment politicians affiliated to or allied with the Hezbollah bloc, which emerged from the elections politically weakened.

To many, the 13 MPs represented the new blood that might help resuscitate Lebanon. Some of these new parliamentarians were friends of mine, activists I have known on the streets of Beirut, people with whom I had marched in protest. Seeing them enter Lebanon's parliament as lawmakers felt surreal. These men and women had once been sprayed with tear gas and fired upon with bullets for protesting against parliament in 2019 and attempting to storm its premises. Now, they entered it proudly.

With their election, there was room for optimism but only a cautious one. Their victory represented a clear political achievement emerging from the 2019 uprising – but it was short of a sweeping triumph.

Today, the way ahead is still bumpy and dangerous. Lebanon is more polarized and divided than ever.

Hezbollah and their allies, supported by Iran, might have lost seats in parliament but they remain strong and dominant. The far-right Lebanese forces, opposed to Hezbollah, and now reportedly funded by Saudi Arabia and the United Arab Emirates, have also gained considerable power. They are two sides that feed off each other in dangerous ways. The country, as it looks now, is divided among those who support Hezbollah and those who want it to be disarmed.

The mainstream parties still represent 90 per cent of parliament. Most Lebanese chose to elect the same old establishment parties that had stripped them of all their rights, including their right to a dignified standard of living. It is hard to explain why. Some people I spoke to were afraid of change amid a crisis. They mainly represent the older civil-war generation that prefers to maintain the status quo. Then, depending on who you ask and their party affiliation, many will blame the other parties for Lebanon's woes and claim their own party is innocent of wrongdoing. Some voters were also discouraged by the divisions and trenchant discourse of the opposition groups, saying their vision was not clear and so they discarded them. Many were also lured by the usual populist rhetoric and sectarian discourse.

I also noticed that many voters actually cast a protest vote rather than an informed one. Their choice was not based on a political party's program per se, instead it was more of a sanction against the political establishment, including when they chose to vote to change their MP. A lot of Christian voters, for instance, cast a vote against Hezbollah rather than for a party standing for real change, which explains why parties like the Lebanese Forces gained power in the last election.

Shia voters remained mostly loyal to Hezbollah. Whether they did so out of conviction or out of fear is another issue. A real revolution against Hezbollah can only start from within and that seems far-fetched at the moment.

The patronage network that the politicians have built throughout the decades still played a role in the elections, despite the economic crisis. Today, 30 per cent of the active population is still employed by the public sector, posts mainly acquired through political and sectarian loyalties. It is hard for these civil servants and their families to break free, especially amid these unprecedented levels of poverty. Leaders can still easily buy their constituency's support; it now takes just a few dollars to do the job. There were reports of vote buying around the country during the elections, especially in its most impoverished areas.

The voter turnout was also lower than expected, with about 50 per cent of the population abstaining. I find it mind-boggling that one would not vote when an opportunity for change presents itself.

The Lebanese lost everything in 2020. If change did not feel imminent then, will it ever? The political elite has successfully managed to reproduce itself. Today's parliament counts among its lawmakers some who are wanted by the law. Two MPs accused in the Beirut explosion of negligence leading to deaths, Ali Hassan Khalil and Ghazi Zaiter of the Shia Amal Party, were re-elected in 2022 and are still using their political immunity to escape justice. They even sit on the judiciary committee in parliament. It could not get more absurd.

There are politicians still in power who contributed to the downfall of our nation, to Lebanese losing their savings, to my daughter being denied a future in Lebanon. There are MPs who have deprived women of their rights. Most members of parliament today still obstruct a woman's right to pass on her nationality to her children. They do not believe that women should be treated equally to men in the workforce, nor that their civil rights should be equal to men. These are misogynist lawmakers who sometimes attack fellow women parliamentarians. New MPs Halima Qaaqour, Cynthia Zarazir, and Paula Yacoubian have been verbally attacked by their male colleagues during legislative sessions. These men will never grant us our rights. Women's rights and empowerment means less power for men and fewer privileges.

For the seventh consecutive time, Nabih Berri, who leads the Shia Amal Party and is an intrinsic pillar of the political establishment, has been re-elected as the Speaker of parliament, albeit with the least number of votes since 1992. He is the longest-serving Speaker in the world. The two MPs accused in the blast probe, Ali Hassan Khalil and Ghazi Zaiter, are from his party. When you understand these connections, you realize that not much is going to change.

When Berri was re-elected as Speaker in May 2022, I was glued to my screen in Paris watching the session. He counted and read out the ballots electing him; they included some protest ballots that read as 'justice for the Beirut blast', 'justice for raped women', 'justice for the depositors', 'justice for Lebanon'. They had been cast by the new MPs. After each of these expressions of justice, Berri repeated 'void'. It was infuriating to see him dismiss these ballots as if they were technically disqualified. His words were just a painful and glaring reflection of the reality we live in. Justice has been cancelled for decades now. Will we ever get it back?

As a journalist, I cannot forget to mention the media's role in all of this impunity. Unfortunately, Lebanon's media has failed to play the role of a watchdog. Traditional mass media outlets are still funded by politicians or businessmen close to them. They are an intrinsic part of the political establishment. When the 2019 uprising started, many media outlets embarked on a suspicious frenzy, offering continuous coverage of the protests and claiming to be a platform for change. But that was short-lived raising question marks about their internal and external agendas. The establishment's money continues to be stronger than the truth.

As this book was being written, parliament had failed to elect, session after session, a replacement for Michel Aoun. Despite the economic crisis, Lebanon has had only a caretaker government, with limited powers, since 2020. Creating a new government in the country is delayed by political parties bickering over their seats in the cabinet, and it often depends on regional developments and jockeying for power by regional groups that hold sway in Lebanon.

In a country with unprecedented economic problems and levels of poverty, the ruling class sees no urgency in forming a new government or electing a new president.

The flawed sectarian power-sharing system, which has contributed to years of political dysfunction, corruption, and patronage, is still defining the rules of the political game. The Taif Agreement, signed and ratified respectively in October and November 1989 by Lebanon's parliament towards the end of the Lebanese civil war, set out plans to transition from a confessional state to a secular one and limit sectarianism to a Senate while abolishing it in parliament. This part of the agreement was never implemented. The political elite has no interest in letting go of the confessional political system.

Lebanon cannot afford to waste any more time. A political vacuum and paralysis means a further degradation of the economic situation. The country urgently needs foreign assistance and that is conditional upon structural change and reforms. But what do you reform? The state does not exist anymore. How do you save the country without radical political change and proper governance? Without an independent judiciary and accountability? The political economy of Lebanon might just continue perpetuating itself without any real overhaul of the system that is now rotten.

The 13 new MPs will not be able to change the country overnight. But if they were to unite as a single bloc, and ally themselves to other lawmakers, they could obstruct the drafting of laws that are detrimental to Lebanon, including on the economy but also on issues of social justice, corruption, and accountability. Unfortunately, the prospects of such unity are slim. Considerable political immaturity has already surfaced among the 13 new MPs and mistakes that are reminiscent of establishment politicians are now also a trait of some of these new parliamentarians.

Lebanon is in crisis. The revolution remains unfulfilled. The future is uncertain.

Was the Beirut explosion also the explosion of Lebanon's modern state? What will it take to save what is left of the country? Its political system has often changed following major violent events. Does Lebanon need a new system and constitution? How do you put in place a new social pact for Lebanon if the same old players are still the dominant force and the new players are immature or divided? How do you fight corruption when it has overtaken the whole system and there is no judiciary left?

How do you deal with and disarm Hezbollah, the elephant in the room, if you want to do it from within?

I have no answers. But I will keep asking the questions.

12

Fighting for Justice

TRACY NAGGEAR

*'But justice is my right, I am not supposed to
fight for justice.'*

Close your eyes for a second and imagine losing the two most important human beings in your life in the span of two years. They are snatched away from you too soon and unjustly. What would you do?

I always wonder if I could have survived being in Tracy's shoes, suffering her tragedies. I would maybe have killed myself or just escaped to the other end of the world where no one and nothing could remind me of the life I once had and the people I loved and lost so suddenly.

Tracy demonstrated great courage, of that there was no doubt. It takes extraordinary strength for a person to endure so much personal loss and yet to keep fighting. It also takes so much devotion to keep working for your country when it has taken everything from you.

I had known Tracy since college days but we had lost contact over the years. The day I found out what happened to her daughter was the day I finally cried after the explosion. I was so numb before I heard the news. I remember locking myself in AP's storage room and weeping for an hour. Her daughter was the same age as mine.

She had the same honey-brown curls as my daughter, the same big hazelnut eyes.

It was only a year later that I had the courage to speak to Tracy. I kept avoiding her story for as long as I could. It was too painful to hear. When I decided to write this book, it became unavoidable.

Tracy and I met a few times as I was working on the book. I visited her whenever I came to Lebanon. We also often exchanged messages on the phone. My interviews with her were always in an apartment in Beit Meri, a mountainous town overlooking Beirut, where she had moved after the explosion.

Before I tell you about Tracy's story on 4 August 2020, I need you to read about what happened on her wedding day. Not many people know that part of her story. And I cannot write about Tracy without going back to that ill-fated day.

'We were home taking pictures. I was taking pictures with my friends and the parents of Paul [her husband] had arrived. I suddenly heard people screaming from the other side of the house, so I ran to see what was happening. My mother was laying down half-conscious on a bench, she was in pain, and mumbling "My head hurts, my heart hurts." My father's cousin, who is a doctor, and who was there, said that she was not breathing well, and we had to call an ambulance. The last thing she told me that day was "No matter what happens, please continue with the wedding." My uncle called me later from the hospital telling me not to be worried, that my mum was just running some tests. He told us to go to the wedding and promised to join in an hour or so. Paul was not aware, I told everybody not to tell him. We got married and right before the party, we were resting in a small room at the venue, I called my uncle. He told me not to worry and that she had to stay overnight at the hospital and could not join the wedding. I told him not to lie to me or I would cancel the wedding. That's when he told me she'd had a heart attack, and she was going to get operated but had a 5 per cent chance of surviving.

'I was shocked, overwhelmed. My father showed up crying, saying he did not know what to do. I removed my wedding dress, though people were waiting for us at the party. Paul wanted us to go to the hospital. But then I thought about it, the last thing my mother said was you continue with the wedding, no matter what. If she ever survived and found out that we cancelled the wedding, she would be upset. It was also not just my party, it's Paul's, his family's, people were already there. She was getting operated for long hours and so I thought it was selfish of me to go to the hospital. I put on the dress again and went down to the party. I put on a fake smile and went on with the night. I was feeling terrible. We stayed for the party and left around two a.m. to the hospital. On our way down, we got a call saying the surgery went well and she was in recovery.

'The next day she was awake, I showed her photos of the night, some videos, we talked. She was super happy that we went through with the wedding. We wanted to plan another small dinner with her when she'd recovered.

'Three days later, she caught a virus at the hospital, apparently, they had a virus in the ICU and she was too weak to fight it. She passed away.'

Tracy now paused, albeit briefly, and smirked.

'Alexandra [Lexou] was born two years later. I remember the first time I saw her, after my C-section, I cried for half an hour. My father thought I had post-partum blues, but I had just realized that I was a mother after I had lost my mother. It was too emotional to be a mother and not to have my mother with me, to realize the love that your mother has towards you. It was difficult but it healed me, it was difficult for me to lose my mother, but the moment I had a daughter she was a saviour honestly.'

Only, Tracy's salvation was short-lived. Losing her mother on her wedding day was not enough – the universe wanted more from her. Alexandra was just four on 4 August 2020. She was playing with her Disney princesses in their apartment in Gemmayzeh overlooking the port in Beirut. She was supposed to have a long life ahead of her.

'After the first explosion went off, we just checked our phones to look for news, but we did not react. You know, we are Lebanese, we are used to this, we just wanted to know who they had killed this time. Paul went to the window and saw the smoke billowing above the port, he told us to come and see. I remember hearing the roar of jetfighters.'

Tracy imitated the sound.

'I remember hearing that whoosh sound you hear in the explosion's videos. But there were airplanes before, I am sure. I told them something weird was happening, that we had to run inside. I ran to carry Alexandra and I remember hearing a sound, and when I turned back I am convinced that I saw a missile falling. I am convinced. I saw it and said shit.'

What about that missile? Aside from the sound of airplanes, which many women, including me, reported hearing, Tracy was the only woman in this book to talk about seeing a missile. According to an article by Bellingcat, the forensic and investigative journalism website, some residents like Tracy might have mistaken a flapping bird for a missile. In Rita's testimony she talked about birds flying out of the port seconds before the big explosion. Of course, nothing is certain, and I am not saying there was no missile, only that there has been no proof of one to this day.

'I was carrying Alexandra and I saw the window blow. We flew away. We flew about six metres. Lexou was still awake, I crawled to protect her. A three-metre door fell on me, and I remember thinking that Lexou was underneath me and so she must be safe. Then I went unconscious.

'Paul and our friend woke up about twenty minutes later. They started looking for us. They could not find us. Then they saw my shoe, there were three doors on top of me, parts of the ceiling and two air-conditioners had pierced my legs. They started to lift everything; it took them fifteen minutes. They woke me up and we woke Lexou up. She looked fine. She had no visible injuries.

'Our friend went down to find an ambulance for me, I was the one badly injured, bleeding, my ribs were broken. He came back and said we had to walk, that outdoors was mayhem, no ambulances were to be found, that it was all dark and devastated. We went six floors down and went to a hospital nearby. It was destroyed. We went to the Red Cross, there was no Red Cross building left. We kept walking and I remember I kept saying that it was the Israelis that had hit us because I was convinced that I had seen a missile. Lexou had started losing consciousness here, I told Paul something was not right, I told him to run and find a hospital. He stopped a motorbike who took Lexou to Saint George Hospital. But the doctor there said they could not help her, so she was taken in an ambulance to another hospital.'

My heart was sinking, aching. I was imagining the scenario, imagining being there, imagining it was my daughter.

'Meanwhile, I could no longer breathe and I was not well at all, so I was taken in a car. I remember that there were no police on the streets, no one, no army, no security officers, it was unbelievable. Media outlets have footage of me going out of the building. The media was there from the beginning, but the army was not there. They didn't come to help, to open the roads, nothing. Why was the media there and not the army? Not the police?

'The blast happened at 6:08 p.m., I made it to a hospital in Beirut at 7:45 p.m. My daughter made it to another hospital a little earlier. But if the army had opened the roads, if our president who knew about the ammonium nitrate and if all these officials had a disaster response in place, things would be different today.'

Tracy told me Alexandra had an oedema in the head, and it grew bigger and bigger with time. She was operated on as soon as they found a hospital but she remained in a coma after that.

'I lost faith in God the day my mother passed away but then when Alexandra was hurt, I was so desperate that I went back to praying, it's all I could do. I had no other choice. I have a friend that called me on the sixth of August saying she had a priest friend who would like to pass by Lexou and pray for her. I consented. Let's try everything.

'He came. What happened inside of the ICU was very weird. He was praying and her heartbeat started going up and down. It was just me, Paul, and him, and no one knows about this by the way. The doctors came in, not understanding what was happening. It looked like she was coming back to life, her heartbeat was going up. The doctors would try and adjust the heart-rate monitor, and it would go up and down. I was on my knees crying, Paul was also crying. The priest himself was in disbelief. The doctors told him to keep going. It was very bizarre. We asked the priest what happened that day, he said one day he would tell us. So, I don't know, some people say you can hear things while in coma. When we used to take Lexou to church, she hated it, she would get scared. Maybe that was it, she was just scared and her heartbeat was reacting to that.'

Tracy paused. I had a knot in my throat.

'I was sure she was going to leave. I was injured at the hospital, sitting on my bed and my friends were surrounding me, and I remember crying and laughing at the same time and saying, "I cannot believe I have to go through this again, it was my mother and then it is my daughter." They were telling me that Lexou's surgery went well but I kept reiterating that my mother's surgery also went well. I told them if she was going to die then I was going to die too. I did not want to live anymore, not after everything I have been through.'

Throughout our conversations, Tracy had what I would describe as a poker face. I knew she was in pain because I knew her story, but not once during our conversations did she really show me much emotion. Even over the phone, she always had this neutrality; ready to answer any question but always with so much composure.

'You lose a mother at twenty-eight years old, that is more normal than losing a four-year-old daughter. I always said that what happened at the wedding is like a movie, losing your mother on your wedding day. But then a bomb struck my house and I lost my daughter, well that is utter madness.'

I asked her how she kept going. I had seen her lead the fight for justice for the past two years. She seemed invincible.

'Paul and I are very strong. We did not take any medication or painkillers since it happened. Even with my injuries, I refused to take anything that might destabilize my emotional state. We had to be fully conscious, we could not get addicted to anything, we had to fight the pain the real way.

'We wanted to leave Lebanon after August 4th. But on the 8th of August, we did our first media interview, though we did not want to. After that, we thought maybe we owed it to our daughter to keep talking about what happened. We saw people's reaction and thought maybe it was better to wait. We postponed our departure again and again, and from then on, the fight for justice began.'

Tracy and her husband lead a victims' committee. It is called the 'August 4' committee. It not only represents victims' families but also the survivors, the injured, and displaced, both Lebanese and foreigners. They organize a protest in front of the port of Beirut every fourth of the month. They have protested in front of officials' homes and judicial courts. They are working with international organizations for justice. Some of the committee's members are resorting to justice in Lebanon while others, with dual nationality, are filing lawsuits from abroad against the Lebanese state. Tracy and her husband have also planned the yearly August 4th commemoration. I was the master of ceremonies in 2021 at their request, speaking on behalf of the victims' families to hundreds of thousands of people.

There are three other committees like theirs: One for the firefighters, known to be close to the Lebanese Forces, another one called 'the martyrs of the port', and a recently formed committee, which split from the latter, and is headed by the brother of one of the victims. That committee has been accused of being manipulated by Hezbollah. Both want the lead prosecutor to be replaced, accusing him of bias.

The four committees don't always come together and have been divided over a variety of issues, including how to work on achieving justice.

'Paul and I didn't go to court here yet,' said Tracy. 'We do believe that some judges here are good and we believe in the bar association, but the problem is that the judiciary is controlled by the political class. So, it does not matter if you have a good judge or good lawyers, they will get rid of them, including killing them. We decided, Paul and I, because Lexou is Canadian and I am Canadian, to go to court in Canada. But we have not been able so far because the blast has not been proven as an act of terrorism yet. But there are Lebanese–French and Lebanese–British resorting to justice in their respective countries. We are working with Legal Action Worldwide and Human Rights Watch and they are helping us. We are asking for an international fact-finding mission. We don't want an international tribunal; we want to know what happened. The Americans and French are not helping us. We asked for satellite images from France. They only gave us images up to 5:50 p.m. They said the satellite was oriented towards Cyprus from 6 to 6:08 p.m. They have footage from all the day, except that period, how come?'

In July 2022, Human Rights Watch wrote an op-ed in the French newspaper *Le Monde* criticizing France and President Emmanuel Macron for obstructing an international investigation under the umbrella of the Human Rights Council. As already mentioned, Macron was the first world leader to visit Beirut following the explosion in August 2020, making promises to help the victims' families and calling for an international investigation. He also proposed a 'political roadmap' to push for reforms, but none of his promises were kept, including support in the quest for justice.

'A central stumbling point comes up in all our conversations: the need for France's green light for other countries to publicly support an investigation mechanism,' said the op-ed. 'The latter seem to defer to France because of the perception of its special relationship with Lebanon, that is to say its colonial history.'

Tracy and other victims said they were angry at the inaction of France and the international community. They felt let down.

'There is an FBI report that says only five hundred tons of ammonium nitrate blew up, but that is not the problem. The problem is where did the rest go? That we need to know. There are a lot of documents missing that the port authorities have. We will never get that.

'What the FBI did was not an investigation. They stayed here for a week. This is not enough. No one questioned us, we are all survivors, we all saw and heard things. No one asked us a question. We are the first witnesses to this explosion. No one spoke to us. Not the Lebanese, not the French, not the Americans. Everyone has political interests. That's what is sad. The international community has let us down. But that does not mean we don't have hope. We believe that with pressure, someone will cave in. Justice is important for me. Justice won't bring back Lexou. But justice is my right, I am not supposed to fight for justice. My daughter was killed, it's her right and my right and the right of every person who had a broken window to know how and why.'

Alexandra has become a symbol in Lebanon. A photo of her on the shoulders of her father in a protest in 2019 carrying a Lebanese flag became an icon in the campaign for the pursuit of justice. I asked Tracy how she felt about that. After all, it is not easy for a mother to see her killed daughter become a poster child.

'I know people have only good intentions, but this is not Lexou. Lexou was a four-year-old child who wanted to play, who loved Mickey and Minney and wanted to go to Disneyland. She was just a baby.'

She paused. I nodded my head in approval.

I asked Tracy about her grieving, as I have only seen her pursue the truth and justice for Alexandra since she was killed. 'Can you grieve before you find justice?' I said.

'I grieve every day. And I will not stop grieving until I find justice. Usually when someone dies in Lebanon, you officially mourn them for a year, you wear black, you don't go out etc. . . . and then you gradually move on. Our grief is perpetually delayed. It has not stopped and it is nowhere near ending. And even then, when justice is served, I am not sure if I will move on. We think about our daughter and bringing her justice every day, every hour, every minute. I will never move on without justice. I can't turn the page without knowing what happened, without getting justice for my daughter. I promised her when she died that those who are responsible will pay for their crime. As long I don't keep my promise, I will not move on.'

Tracy was still not giving me any emotions. Unlike most of the women in this book, she never shed a tear. It always felt like there was a screen between us that I couldn't seem to penetrate.

In retrospect, I realize now it wasn't that she didn't have any emotions. She was just a bitter and sardonic woman who was hurting and angry. Her sombre features mirrored her endless pain.

'Two years on, we are still grieving. We still don't go out, we don't celebrate our birthdays, or any holidays, because we are still mourning.

'I still wake up and cry every day. Mornings are the toughest. Every morning you wonder if it was a nightmare or not, it hits you. Mornings are also calm, so it's the time when you are alone. I look at her photos and cry. At night, I sleep, at least now I do. At first, I used to wake up at six a.m. and wonder where she was. I would remember she was gone and could not go back to sleep. Then I got worse, I would wake up even earlier, at two a.m. and three a.m. It is only recently that I started sleeping again.'

When we met in February 2022, to my surprise Tracy was pregnant with a baby boy and was about to give birth. She said this wasn't planned. Both Tracy and her husband were not sure they wanted another kid, at least not so quickly. But the news felt like a glimmer of light in the darkness they lived in. Tracy initially wanted to deliver her baby in Paris as it was safer for them due to the collapse of Lebanon's health sector, but she changed her mind.

'I just did not feel it. I also thought that I was due in March [2022] and there are parliamentary elections in Lebanon in May [2022], and I want to be there. I can't run away from Lebanon. I'll take the risk one more time, one last time. I thought I couldn't take it, that I would leave Lebanon and would be traumatized. But I didn't care. I continued the fight; I took the risk and I take risks every day. My priority is justice.'

Tracy and Paul were also involved in politics. With their three-year-old Alexandra in tow, they had taken part in the protests of 2019. Paul ran for the order of the engineers in 2021 against the establishment's political parties and won. The couple also campaigned and supported independent candidates in Lebanon's 2022 parliamentary elections, many of whom were activists on the streets during the uprising. Thirteen new MPs, outsiders to the political establishment, were admitted to parliament in 2022, an unexpected result. But Tracy and I agreed that it was not enough.

'Everyone talks about these elections being the beginning of change, but we have no time for gradual change. We lost everything; these elections were supposed to be the end of the current political establishment. If, after the bankruptcy of the state, the port explosion, after people lost their deposits, after Lebanon's collapse, we can still not get a majority in parliament, then when will we? There cannot be more favourable conditions for change and yet many chose to elect the very same politicians who led us to our demise. People don't want change.'

Before the elections, Tracy told me that the parliamentary race would be decisive in her decision to leave or stay in Lebanon. I called her after the elections. She had given birth to her son Axel, named after Alexandra.

'Truth is we have not decided yet. It is a difficult choice as we are still fighting for justice and for Alexandra. But we don't feel secure here and we don't feel alive anymore.

'Since Axel's birth, we are happier and more serene but it is nothing like before August 4th. Everything here reminds us of August 4th and of Lexou. I cannot have my son live that life. He needs some normalcy. We cannot punish him and deny him a normal life. He might also get killed tomorrow, it's a huge risk. Lebanon is not a place to raise children anymore. There is no future here. The country is insupportable. No power, no internet, no fuel, no food. People are queuing for bread for God's sake.'

Every Christmas since Alexandra's death, Tracy and Paul organize an online fundraising, to cook and distribute hot meals to thousands of Lebanese families during the holidays. They call it Alexandra's initiative. I find it incredible that they still have the will to give back to Lebanon despite what happened to them.

'It's a matter of time before we go. We are thinking of dividing our time between Lebanon and France, maybe test life abroad but still give Lebanon another year. We have two children after all. We owe it to Axel to provide him with the best life, but we owe it to Lexou not to let go of our fight for justice. We also want to keep contributing to change; educating people about better political choices. We are afraid that if we leave Lebanon for good, we could forget about this.

'We lost our daughter, our house. It would be difficult to accept the idea that they also managed to kick us out of our country at the end.'

At the end of 2022, Tracy and her husband finally moved back to their apartment in Beirut where Alexandra was killed on 4 August 2020. Tracy shared a photo of the before and after scene on social media with the following text:

'We thought of leaving to feel less pain. But our people came together, rebuilt the city with zero help, and gave us hope and the strength to fight. So, we fought and will do so until our last breath. You can throw your tear gas, bullets or ammonium nitrate. We will resist you. This is our land and we will claim it. Two years later, we are finally back . . .'

The entrance of their apartment now has a neon light that reads 'Alexandra's home'.

TATIANA HASROUTY

'I don't want our politicians to stay. I want to change everything, and I want justice.'

'On August 4th, I lost my father, he was everything to me. I lost my home as well. Our apartment was damaged. When the explosion happened, I was sleeping. I lost my safe space. I lost Lebanon. As a law student, as Tatiana, I want to make sure that this won't happen again. I don't want our politicians to stay. I want to change everything, and I want justice.'

She was just 21, one of the youngest women in this book. But Tatiana's maturity and resolve meant she knew exactly what she wanted and would go to great lengths to get it. When we first met in 2021, she was still a law student finishing her bachelor's degree. I had seen her on international media outlets and in protests by the families of victims, but it was a social media post of hers, on international women's day, that caught my attention. It was a picture of her with the Beirut port in the background and she was wearing a shirt that read 'Women can move mountains.'

Tatiana came across as a smart young woman who was engaged in her fight for justice, not just for her father's death and the other victims but also for women's rights.

'I'm happy that you're doing a book with women only,' she said to me as soon as I told her about the project when I visited her in the summer of 2021.

'I come from a mid to low socio-economic class, I belong to a marginalized community of women. Lebanon gave us nothing but we sacrificed our families, our homes, and now our country. My maternal grandmother lost a son in the civil war, lost her daughter because of child marriage, and now her son-in-law died, all of it because of this country. What did she do to deserve all of this? And she buried everything in her heart and to this day she has no healthcare, no retirement fund, nothing. From a young age I realized there's no equality, nothing is fair. Not just between men and women, but between us and other women. I was never rich but I had the opportunity to learn, to go to school, and I always had this revolution within me against injustice so I decided to become a lawyer.'

Tatiana's father, who was a worker at the infamous grain silos of the Beirut port, was killed on 4 August 2020. He had been the main breadwinner of the family. Tatiana had been consumed with rage ever since.

'He worked at the Beirut port for thirty-eight years. I get angry because he spent all his life at the port. He was about to retire. He didn't spend much time with us, his children, he didn't see us grow up and was waiting for his retirement to spend time with us. I feel disappointed, I knew that our state is bad but not this much. I lost my person in the house.'

Tatiana started tearing up. I stayed silent.

'On August 4, at 5:30 p.m., he called my mother saying he was not coming home and needed someone to get him a blanket and a pillow so he can sleep at work because they had been expecting a wheat ship late that night. That was the last phone call with dad. If anyone had actually gone down to give him the pillow and blanket, they would have died. We didn't know exactly how far the warehouse number 12 was from him. His colleagues, those who survived, told us that everyone knew something shady was happening in that warehouse. That no one was allowed in. But, he saw the fire and didn't leave, maybe he felt safe underneath the silos. He used to tell my mother that during the war he wasn't scared from bombs, the grain silos protected him.'

This time the silos didn't, but they might have shielded Beirut from further damage.

The infamous grain silos at the Beirut port, though partly damaged by the blast, were still standing in 2022. Many believe they actually contained part of the pressure and spared the city further damage. They are the only structure left at the port acting as a reminder of what happened on that day. They have come to symbolize the crime committed against Beirut and its people.

In April 2022, and despite the fierce opposition of the victims' families, the Lebanese government issued a decision to demolish the silos, citing an expert report that said they posed a danger and were too costly to be renovated. Ever since, women like Tatiana, Tracy, and others have been mobilizing to stop that from happening.

When I visited Lebanon in the summer of 2022, smoke was rising from the surroundings of the silos. The structures had reportedly caught fire from the fermented wheat left there since 2020. The silos burnt for almost two months and no effort was made to extinguish the fire. The authorities claimed that water would trigger their collapse. The families of victims accused the government of instigating and maintaining the fire so as to eventually trigger the collapse of the remaining structure.

Ironically, on the second anniversary of the explosion, on 4 August 2022, as Lebanese people marched passed the port to remember the darkest day of their lives, part of the structure collapsed. A thick and toxic cloud covered the port and the surrounding area, triggering the unhealed traumas of that day.

'This is a crime scene. These silos also somehow represent us and our families, despite everything and despite the explosion they are still standing strong. This was also my father's second home. But most importantly, we are worried that people will just forget if these silos are gone. This political class keeps committing crimes and erasing the evidence. We don't want that to happen.'

Tatiana's father went missing for 14 days following the blast, his body lying somewhere around those silos. For two agonizing weeks she was trapped in a false sense of hope, expecting him to show up at the door again.

'My brother-in-law went down to the port to look for him that night. They did not allow him in and said they could not look for him or anyone else, before they got help, mainly from the French search and rescue team.

'I really thought he was hiding somewhere, I thought maybe he said to his team, let's go under the tunnels. There were underground tunnels where he used to hide during the civil war. We kept thinking my father and his colleagues were hiding somewhere. We waited and waited, no updates from the government. I ended up contacting a French general working with the rescue mission. I emailed him, and he replied and provided me with daily updates.

He asked me to send photos of my father to identify him, he helped us more than the Lebanese government. A Lebanese official called us 14 days later to tell us that the DNA matched and they found my dad's body. I dreamt that night that my family was waiting for me to wake up and when I woke I saw him and he was wearing his usual clothes, a stripped beige T-shirt with brown pants. I hugged him and told him, "Where were you? We were looking for you! How come you didn't show up?" He didn't talk to me. He hugged me and I kept saying, "Where were you? Why didn't you show up before? We were looking for you, please come back."'

Tatiana was crying. Her sorrow stung my heart to the core, but I was incapable of shedding tears this time. I didn't know if I had become inured to sorrow after so many interviews or this was just my coping mechanism at work.

'He wanted to see me graduate. Instead he died. I'm a bit relieved because he didn't feel any pain before dying. Or at least I hope. Everything I wanted to do with him I did it. I told him I loved him, I told him "Thank you." Maybe it's a consolation, I am not sure.'

I asked her if her fight for justice was bringing her any solace.

'The port was my dad's second home; his colleagues were his family. He would have done everything for them. I'm doing the same for him, for his family, for Lebanon. I don't want anyone to live what I lived through, for a daughter to grow up without her father. I don't want little girls to die before they can achieve anything. I couldn't find my father for 14 days and even when I did, I had no closure. I still have no closure. Who did it? Why? And why did my dad pass away? What for? My father gave a lot to Lebanon during the war, he worked at the grain silos, with wheat. If he stopped working no one would eat bread. He gave Lebanon his life, I think it's time to repay him.'

Tatiana was not officially involved in the various victims' committees. She was aware of the divisions and issues in each committee and preferred not to commit to them, but she took part in their events and actively participated in the various protests.

She was one of the few young Lebanese to meet the UN Secretary General António Guterres personally during his visit to Lebanon in 2022. She asked him for an international fact-finding mission.

'We don't want an international tribunal. We just want to know what happened, this is the first step.'

As a young lawyer, Tatiana understood that the road to justice in Lebanon was paved with bad intentions, but it didn't stop her from fighting.

'My family appointed a lawyer and from the beginning, we asked the bar association to defend us. The Lebanese bar association has been actively defending the victims of August 4th.'

The bar association's former head, the lawyer Melhem Khalaf, had become one of the new members of parliament. Many victims' families hoped his election would give justice some momentum.

'But in Lebanon everything is complicated, justice is not going to happen anytime soon, that I know,' Tatiana added, almost as if to remind herself of the grim reality.

'I trusted Judge Sawan, he used to teach me at the university. I know he's very transparent and respectful. A judge should have a message and Judge Sawan has one.'

Tatiana was referring to Judge Fadi Sawan, the first prosecutor assigned to investigate the explosion, but he was removed from his position only a few months after his appointment. A court decided he was not suitable for the position, after two ministers whom he had accused of criminal negligence filed a complaint against him. The court decision was also partly based on the fact that Judge Sawan's home was itself damaged in the blast, so his position as lead prosecutor represented a conflict of interest.

'We all know that is not why they removed him. They will find any excuse to impede justice. I hope that Judge Bitar will be like Sawan.'

Judge Bitar was the new prosecutor in the probe into the explosion. His work had also been challenged by a series of lawsuits filed against him by those politicians being accused as part of the investigation. He had not been able to do much work since his nomination.

'He has the responsibility to bring justice for the victims, the family's victims and the people who were traumatized. He will not bring back the people who died, but it's a step towards a better Lebanon. When people take responsibility for their mistakes, it will stop others from doing the same.'

Accountability – what a futile concept in a place like Lebanon. Very few politicians have been put on trial in recent history and gone to jail. Parliament was still trying in 2022 to pass a motion to transfer the explosion probe from the prosecutor to the Supreme Council for the trial of presidents and ministers. But this is a judicial body in charge of political impeachment which has never tried a minister, president, or lawmaker. It was created to protect them, not to punish them.

'They are manoeuvring to undermine the probe and manipulate any accountability mechanism. The judge's work has also been obstructed by the series of suspension requests. These will lead nowhere but they are slowing down the probe, allowing those in power to buy time. The next step for the judge is to issue a preliminary verdict charging those responsible and then their trial begins, but this has not happened yet.'

Politicians in Lebanon can easily block a judge's career and influence his position and upward mobility. They directly interfere in the nominations of judges. But that didn't stop Tatiana from wanting to work in Lebanon one day. She was keen on contributing to changing the judiciary and giving back to her community. But first, she aspired to go abroad to continue her education. Unfortunately, that partly depended on financial resources which had gone dry since her dad passed away.

'My dad had a life insurance but it has still not paid. They say they want to know what officially caused the explosion first. That will never happen soon. He also has an end-of-service retirement salary from social security. They didn't want to give it to us either.

It's not much but it helps us survive. His retirement savings would have been much more had the currency not collapsed. My mother cried and told them she had to pay for my university fees, the house expenses. They ended up giving us the money but it was in the form of a bank cheque and the bank forced us to freeze the money for six months because of the financial crisis. It was infuriating because that was our compensation money. Even after we had been through so much, we still had to beg for it. I told them I had to pay for my tuition. They eventually accepted to transfer my university fees only, but kept freezing the rest.'

Tatiana voted for the first time in the parliamentary elections in 2022. In Lebanon, the voting age is not before 21. You can drive and drink at 18, as a woman you can even get married as early as 14, but you have no right to cast a ballot before you are 21.

'I voted for change but I am surprised people are still supporting the same old political parties. With everything that has happened to us, many still believe in them. Someone was arguing with my mother that the president shouldn't be blamed for what happened on August 4 because he's old and he could not have done much, so we can't blame him. She said if he's 87, if he can't rule a country, then he should quit. Some of my family members were upset about what she said. People don't have clear priorities, they can't see what's wrong and this is what upsets me. Some people will come to us saying don't speak about Hezbollah, you will be killed. For me it doesn't matter anymore, if they want to kill me let them kill me.'

I asked Tatiana if her father ever spoke about the notorious corruption at the port, since he spent most of his life there.

'My grandfather used to work at the port as well, they had a policy that the father that works there can hire his son. We thank God that my brother didn't go to work there even when we insisted he did. My dad used to tell us that political parties just hired whoever they wanted there, most people had ghost jobs and never showed up to work. My father was never appointed by a party, he was just a dedicated worker. They kept him there because he did well and he did not interfere with the political parties' manoeuvres there, he just did his job and kept silent.'

In the summer of 2022, Tatiana and I met again. She seemed a little less overwhelmed and somehow happier. We had a coffee at a famous café in Gemmayzeh that had been completely destroyed in the explosion. The place was now back on its feet and busy with customers.

'I will never rest because it's a government who failed us, a country that failed us and is still doing it. They asked me how I would judge them, those responsible, since I am a lawyer now. I said I won't kill them, I won't end their lives. It's not my decision to end anyone's life, just like they didn't have the right to end my father's life. If they are criminals, I'm not a criminal and I will never be because of them. I want them to be punished, I want them to live what we lived through.

'No political leader said "I failed you, I couldn't provide for this country, because I didn't know how to do it." We went down to the streets after the blast, we were angry, the police showered us with tear gas and rubber bullets. People were beaten up and injured for asking for justice, after their houses were destroyed and their loved ones killed. Can you imagine? But the next day it was over and it was business as usual. We are going through the worst days in our history, and for us, the victims' families, it cannot be business as usual.'

HIAM KAABOUR

'The Lebanese state killed my son, I accuse it of killing my son.'

I went to see Hiam in the summer of 2021. She lived in an impoverished area of Beirut close to the country's largest football stadium which was built in the 1950s and once hosted the football Asian Cup in 2000. Now it lay deserted, decaying with time.

It was not hard to find her apartment. A giant poster of her son Ahmad, a young man with brown hair and sharp green eyes, was hanging on the balcony.

Hiam is known as 'Om Ahmad' or 'mother of Ahmad'. Women in Lebanon and the Arab world use their son's first name, the eldest in the case of more than one, to refer to themselves. Their husbands do the same. It is a patriarchal custom at best, a son has a special status in the family. You would almost never find parents calling themselves after the first name of their daughter.

Om Ahmad once had a son, now she only had a daughter.

'I was married at a young age, I was fifteen. I had my children Nadine and Ahmad when I was young. I raised them and educated them like any other mother. It was hard first because I was a young mother. I really suffered. In Lebanon, it is even more difficult to have a child and to provide for them a proper life. At that time, my husband was unemployed, and our situation was bad. It was the end of the war, I gave birth during the Aoun wars. I suffered a lot, I was always hiding in the shelters.'

Om Ahmad was referring to the wars that the former Lebanese president, Michel Aoun, who was in power during the blast, fought at the end of the civil war against his Christian rivals and then against Syria.

'I got married during the war, I gave birth during the war, and I raised my kids during the war. I raised them in poverty and misery, this is Lebanon. This is Aoun, from the day I gave birth until this day. Michel Aoun is still here. He killed my son. All the corrupt ruling class without any exception killed our children. They are all criminals, murderers! And they will keep committing their crimes because there is no justice.

'I raised my son; he became a young man. I was so happy when he graduated from school. Ahmad's goal was to be a civil servant, as simple as that. At eighteen, he applied many times to become an officer in the state security agency, then tried at the general security and the police, it didn't work out. We didn't have any connections; we didn't know anyone and they asked us for money. Where would I get money to bribe the state for the job. He decided to continue university, and then look for a job. Unfortunately, in this country if you don't have connections, you can't get anything. In Lebanon it's all about political affiliations, you know a politician, you find a way. Thank God we are not affiliated with any party. Ahmad didn't manage to find work, he lost hope and decided to immigrate. We didn't want him to leave, he was our only son, I wanted him to stay with me. He started to fight with his dad about leaving and he applied to Canada without telling us. He was young and wanted an opportunity to live. His last job was in accounting, he worked for a sweets and ice cream company in Hamra, Beirut. When the uprising started in 2019 and later with the Covid-19 pandemic, he was fired from his job. He decided to work as a taxi driver, but it was not going well because of the fuel crisis. Nothing worked out for him. He insisted on leaving the country, he got accepted for immigration to Canada. He had an interview at the Canadian Embassy on August 22. They killed him on August 4th. He left us, but not to Canada, he left us to a place with no return. I wish he went to Canada, how I wish.'

Om Ahmad was wearing a thick black veil. Her whole outfit was black, like most of the mourning women I met. Her husband was sitting with us, he wiped away his tears. They both looked frail and like they had aged so much since Ahmad was lost to them.

'A wall fell from the 4th floor of an adjacent building on the driver's seat, where he was sitting. On the seat next to him, there was a box with a cake, the cake was unharmed.'

Om Ahmad was sobbing. It was a familiar sight. I sat there and waited, as usual. The women were often crying and talking at the same time.

'I saw my son drowned in his own blood, I took him in my arms and talked to him . . . he did not answer. This keeps playing in my head non-stop.

'In the hospital Ahmad was left alone, laying on the floor, covered with blood. No one was helping him. He needed urgent help. I kept on screaming asking for help. No one helped us. People with connections got hospitalized, they are the same people who got the work opportunities that Ahmad never got. Everything works with connections.

'At 9:30 p.m., three hours and a half later, they took him for surgery, but it was too late.

'He entered the operation room but there were no surgeons available, he was treated by a general doctor. Did they kill him? Did they fail to treat him properly? I think so. I hope that God does not forgive them. Ahmad left us and took everything with him.'

The day before we met, Om Ahmad took part in a protest outside the home of the caretaker interior minister, who was barring the lead prosecutor, Judge Tarek Bitar, from questioning Lebanon's head of General Security, General Abbas Ibrahim, over the explosion. About 100 people, including Om Ahmad, marched towards the minister's apartment in Beirut holding empty coffins and hurling them in front of the building. Some protesters even tried to storm the building and sprayed the word 'killer' on the entrance door. Police fired tear gas on the protesters who refused to leave, scuffling with the security forces. Many people were injured.

'They are all criminals. I'm just asking for justice, is that too much? For the criminals to be prosecuted, all of them without any exceptions. I want the prosecution to start from the president. The president knew about the ammonium nitrate and did nothing. He claims he had no prerogatives or power to intervene. Fuck prerogatives. There were explosives in the middle of the city, and you failed to act. Every leader in the government is also guilty. I don't want them to go to prison, or to die. I want their kids to die and for them to feel the pain and torture that I'm feeling. This is a state of sectarian political parties, of assassins. During the war with Israel, Israel the enemy, things were not like that. We were not hungry, we were not humiliated, and our kids didn't die in hospitals. People weren't fighting for fuel; we didn't stay all day without electricity. The war with Israel is not even close to the war that political leaders have waged against us. The president warned us, saying we were going to hell. I hope that he goes to hell. We know that we won't go to hell, but he will. In Israel, if the sound of a bullet is heard the government warns the citizens to hide. Here, our leaders killed us, our government killed us, burned us. The Lebanese state killed my son, I accuse it of killing my son.'

Om Ahmad was bursting with rage. The veins in her forehead were bulging.

'I'm asking all the countries, Europeans, Arabs, to come and take our leaders because they will keep killing us. We tried to get rid of them, but we cannot. It's a mafia with too many heads. There is nothing moving forward in Lebanon. They have taken us hostage. They are taking justice hostage. They starved us and killed us, what else? And at the same time, our leaders find and buy medicine, their kids still live a luxurious life and they are happy. Our kids are buried, and their kids are living. No! We cannot keep being silent anymore. Our kids will not be buried for their kids to live. And if there is no justice, we are going to take revenge with our hands. I will not let this go. The day will come and they will see.'

I asked her who she planned to go after, there were so many after all. Ministers, heads of security agencies, presidents.

'All of them. All of them. It is not just me who has not been harmed by them. Even you. If you didn't die from the explosion, you will die from the lack of medication or from hunger. They stole everything from us, killed us, made us poor, and made us beg. If the army just retreats from the streets, takes our side, then you will see what will happen to them. We will cut them in pieces. I swear, I swear, I will cut them in pieces. I lost everything I have; I don't have anything to lose anymore. He means everything to me, my prince, they took him from me. Why? Was he fighting against Israel? He was working to provide for himself. He worked to provide for us. What was he doing?

Their hands are smeared with blood of my son. Not only my son but all the victims. Who transported the ammonium nitrate to the port? Who in Lebanon has arms and fights? They're afraid to say that it is Hezbollah. Who else would bring and store explosives in the country? Who was bringing the ammonium nitrate and using it to attack Syria? Why don't they say who's the party behind this? However, both the party and the state are to blame because Hezbollah brought it with state approval. It's the Lebanese government who brought the nitrate to the port They killed our children. They bombed Beirut. They killed us.

'You live all your life for your children, you live to see them grow up and become adults. At the end they bring them to you in a coffin. This is Lebanon.'

She paused. A painful silence ensued.

I told her Ahmad was a very handsome man. I felt stupid for saying that. But I was speechless and helpless in the face of her wrath. To my surprise she smiled and calmed down a bit.

I asked her if I could take a photo of the table next to me. There was a Quran with Ahmad's photos as a baby. He was blond with a silky bang dropping onto his forehead. She approved.

'He was the moon in its fullness. I swear, I was hiding him from people. He was beautiful with rose-coloured cheeks, green eyes, and blond hair. I hid him from people's eyes. Now I hide him underground. Where no one can ever see him again. Not even me. Where will they hide their kids tomorrow? I hope they burn in hell. Allah, listen to me, I hope they burn with their kids in hell. I know where my kid is. But do they know what their fate is? The day will come, and they will stand in front of Allah and they will be judged. I hope that all the Lebanese leaders, from the oldest to the youngest, are sent to hell.'

PART FOUR

Death of a Nation?

Lebanon might not be dead yet, but the Lebanon we have known is definitely fading away. It is in a comatose state without any proper care.

The international community is refusing to help Lebanon without any structural changes. The country is plunging deeper into what seems like a bottomless abyss. Anywhere you look, people are merely surviving. Lebanon has been left by its politicians to slowly perish. For three years since the onset of the economic crisis, Lebanon's leaders have wasted time, depleted foreign currency reserves without any proper reforms. Millions of people are unemployed, shortages of food and medicine are still widespread. Lebanon's people seem to have given up too. No one protests on the streets anymore. People are consumed by their daily struggles, fighting to feed their children, adjusting, without changing much. For the victims of 4 August 2020 the absence of justice means the process of grieving is endlessly delayed. Lebanon is a nation that isn't healing. The mass exodus of Lebanese to other countries has irreversible consequences for the future of the country. What will Lebanon look like in the future? If it survives, or resuscitates, will it ever go back to what it once was? Can a new Lebanon be born? A better one? Or has Lebanon turned into an endlessly failed state, another pariah in the region?

13

Slowly Dying

LARA EL KHOURY

*'But it is so hard. She is not dead but she is
not alive either.'*

Lara's story, like that of all the women in this book, is Lebanon's story. Hers specifically represents the slow and agonizing death of Lebanon. The country, as we once knew it, is slowly disappearing, and we are mourning it every day. We are mourning what is no more, what we have lost and keep losing.

I read about Lara in a local newspaper in the aftermath of the explosion. Lara, who is now 45, had been in a coma since the Beirut explosion. As in the case of Liliane, she was not able to tell her own story.

Her mother Najwa and I met for the first time in the autumn of 2021, then again in the summer of 2022. Lara's situation was deteriorating and Najwa was painfully having to watch her slowly die day after day.

'Her head was injured, one of her eyes is gone and her ears were hurt. We didn't know if she could hear well or not, even the doctors didn't know. But she was responsive at first. I was talking to her, and I felt like she was listening to me. Her eyes were glowing as if she was listening to me. I was happy to see her respond to me. They could move her, move her legs. Now her muscles are thawing, her bones are melting, even her skin is rotting. She is just a corpse breathing. Her legs are like wooden sticks, they need to carry her to move her and change her diapers. Her hands are twisted, and her palms don't open.'

Najwa imitated Lara's hands, clenching her fists, turning them inwards.

'My heart is made of stone now, I can't even cry anymore. I sometimes pinch myself to feel. There is anger, maybe hatred mixed with sadness. One day I blame God, one day I blame destiny, one day I blame the government. Why? Why her? And in this house?'

Lara was home in her mother's apartment in Achrafieh in Beirut on 4 August 2020. Her brain was completely damaged in the explosion. She'd been lying in a comatose state at a rehabilitation centre outside of Beirut ever since.

'I have reached a stage where I've lost hope. I don't want her to be in pain anymore, she's fading away and I'm breaking down because I can't do anything for her. Her medical record says her brain was damaged. How will she wake up? A miracle?'

Najwa smiled sarcastically.

'Imagine seeing your adult daughter being changed every two hours, like a baby, it's heartbreaking.'

Najwa visited Lara every single weekend after 4 August 2020.

'I took a permission to sleep next to her. I sit with her from Friday until Sunday. I am not allowed to be there longer. I talk to her, tell her stories, try to refresh her memory, make her listen to music. I put nail polish on her nails every time I go, she loved keeping her nails neat.

'I don't sleep when I am with her. She doesn't either. She can feel me. The doctors say she still has a reflex and that is why she can still react. When she hears my voice, her eye moves. I talk to her until four a.m., I hug her and kiss her. I feel like she's comfortable with me. But it is so hard. She is not dead but she is not alive either. I miss her and I want to talk to her. I sometimes feel like shaking her, I tell her "Wake up, wake up, you cannot stay like this, you cannot accept this. You never liked sleeping." I go crazy. I come back home feeling sick.

'Every time I visit her, I come back crying.'

Najwa stood up and told me to come with her. She took me to Lara's room. She opened an oblong closet covered with a mirror to show me her outfits. Everything looked untouched. There were photos of her and her friends next to her bed, and to my surprise I spotted a good friend of mine there who was apparently her former co-worker.

Time had somehow managed to stop in Lara's room.

'I made sure it still looked the same, if she is ever back.'

Najwa sat on Lara's bed. She looked lonely and powerless.

'It's very hard, very hard, and I don't feel like this is my house anymore. My daughter was young, full of life.

'She loved Lebanon. She was a patriot at heart. She loved the freedom in Lebanon, the weather of Lebanon, the vibrant social life in it. She took part in the protests in 2019, she was proud. She never wanted to leave her country. But look at Lebanon now, it is vanishing too and they are letting it struggle and agonize. This is what hurts the most. They are watching it die.'

Lebanon, just like Lara, was on life support. And both of them might probably never wake up.

Najwa got up to check if the power in the house was back on. She put the fan on. It was a balmy July afternoon. Beirut's residents have no electricity most days and air-conditioning units don't always function with private generators. The voltage isn't high enough.

'We pay for a private generator but with high fuel prices they turn it on only a few hours a day. As soon as it is on, I try to finish all the house chores.'

Najwa lived by herself, for her husband passed away at the end of 2019. I asked her what it was like being alone, now that Lara, who had lived with her, was gone.

'I talk to the mirror.'

She laughed.

'I come back from work exhausted, I eat, and I do my laundry. I
turn on the television, I lay down, I speak to my sister or friends. I
talk to Lara before sleeping, I come to her room and speak to her.
My life became boring, it is ugly.

'My son has a daughter, he's getting upset because I'm not there
for him. But I'm broken. I go to the hospital and spend 48 hours
sitting on a couch looking at my daughter in this vegetative state.
And then I have to go see my granddaughter and play with her and
pretend. I have to play two roles, it's so difficult, and I try to hide
my suffering because I know how much my son loves his sister
and is attached to her. But I can't go from the hospital directly to
him, I need my time. Even though I take my stuff with me, I take
a shower, I prepare myself. But still I can't go out from the hospital
directly to see my grandchild, it just does not feel right.'

I expected Najwa to be retired now that she was 70. But she still
worked full-time as a personal assistant in a bank in Beirut. Lara's
care at the hospital cost her about 1,700 USD a month. She had no
means to cover that by herself, especially with the devaluation of
the Lebanese pound. She had been relying on the support of donors
and organizations. That help could have stopped at any moment.

'Of course, the ministry of health is bankrupt and won't help.
No official asked about us anyway. We are Orthodox Christians,
even our own church did not help. It was Islamic organizations
who came and cleaned the building, distributed relief aid. I am
still working because I have to. I have to keep earning an income
because I am using and depleting my retirement fund to pay for
her hospital fees. I also cannot stay home alone. If I stay home
alone for a day, I get depressed. I go to her room and start looking
into her stuff. At night I hear her talking to me, I imagine her
walking in the house.'

Najwa said she didn't have an easy relationship with Lara. The
two grew apart when Najwa and her husband had to leave Lebanon
during the war to work in Nigeria and then Saudi Arabia. Lara and
her brother were raised by Najwa's parents and her sister.

'I didn't get the chance to be close to her, and our circumstances didn't help. I used to visit them frequently but it wasn't enough. When she graduated from school I moved back to Lebanon. She started her university studies in education for children with special needs. She graduated from university and I settled in Lebanon. I wanted to be close to her but it was too late. She had her own life, her friends, and her work. Every time I tried to be closer, we fought. I struggled a lot with her. She had a difficult divorce and then loved a man who was not good for her.'

Najwa paused.

'I even miss fighting with her. I wish she would come back and we would fight.'

Lara worked as an HR manager before the explosion, but her dream was to open her own business one day. She was passionate about children and wanted to have a nursery in Beirut.

'She had no children of her own. Maybe that's better when I think about it now. But Lara worked with children with special needs for a while. She loved kids. She didn't have a successful marriage, so I wanted her to accomplish herself through her career. I wanted to support her financially, but the economic crisis in Lebanon didn't help and her father passed away end of 2019.'

I asked Najwa if she lived with the fear of losing Lara. I was always scared to ask about her daughter whenever I texted her.

'Every time the phone rings I panic. But I have reached a point where I am wishing she would just rest in peace, that I would lose her instead of seeing her like this, disfigured, lifeless. I refuse to remember Lara like that. I already feel like I lost her.

'I keep thinking to myself, how did I lose my daughter in ten minutes? In ten minutes they destroyed our city and we lost our country and we cannot complain to anyone, that's what's tragic about our story.'

Lara was still in a coma at the beginning of 2023.

14

Grief

SARAH COPELAND

'How do you parent a child after they are dead?'

'Somehow the sun still rises every day. Somehow it still sets. But life as I know it stopped at 6:08 p.m. on August 4th and that is where part of me remains.'

These were the words of Sarah Copeland written on her personal blog Sarah Yvonne (https://sarah-yvonne.com) a few months after losing her son Isaac to the Beirut explosion. He was not even three. A shred of glass tore through his tiny chest while he was eating dinner at home that evening. He succumbed to his injury a few hours later.

I first got to know Sarah through her writing. The Australian mother had been vocal about her grief, turning her pain into words, blogging about her journey since losing Isaac, the youngest victim of the explosion on 4 August 2020.

'Today, the grief feels like a heavy weight that I carry around. I walk through this world like my head is in a fog and my legs are made of lead. The air feels thick and I have to move slowly and deliberately to push my way through,' she wrote on another blog post.

I interviewed her the first time online for a story I wrote for the AP to mark the six-month anniversary of the explosion. She had already returned to Australia. We stayed in touch afterwards and spoke a few times after that.

'What happened to us is so unreal. The way Isaac died is so hard to wrap one's head around, to understand. I imagined the worse when he was born. I did think about the bad things that could happen to him. But what happened featured nowhere in my imagination. I still can't believe that this is our story. But the more time goes on, the more is the growing realization that he is not coming back, and then that is a whole new type of grief, realizing that this is it.'

Sarah said her grief had not been linear. It was a rollercoaster of emotions that took her up and down, every day, every hour, every minute.

'It just becomes different. It's gone from that initial shock to now the creeping realization that this is it.

'I am also angry. You would think that the main anger is towards Lebanese politicians and authorities, but it's not. There is definitely some of that but the main anger is towards myself. I think that is the hardest. I keep thinking that the only reason we were in Lebanon is because of my job. I feel a lot of guilt. I go over every single detail about that night.

'It was a hot day and we had these glass doors added to the balcony and the glass door was half open to let a tiny bit of air come in. I wonder if I should have opened it further, he wouldn't have been exposed to the glass. I wonder what I could have done differently that would have saved him. I carry the guilt of all the little things that led to that exact moment.'

On 4 August, Sarah had come home to her apartment in Sursock street in Achrafieh from the United Nations headquarters in downtown Beirut, where she had been working for a year.

'I set him up for dinner. I was sitting with him, and funny I remember what he was eating. It was chicken and couscous and he had been throwing it on the floor. I was telling him not to do that and he was getting upset.

'I can't even eat couscous anymore.

'I was trying to settle him down by playing some nursery rhymes, it was either Alouette or Baby Shark. He used to change the names of the sharks to the names of the girls in daycare with him.'

Sarah started tearing up. I couldn't see it clearly on the screen but I could hear it in her voice.

'Isaac died not long after we got to the hospital. But the doctors asked Craig not to tell me because they were worried about my pregnancy.'

Sarah was six months pregnant on 4 August, expecting a brother for Isaac.

'I never got to say goodbye. Or "I love you" or any of that.'

Only on the next morning did Sarah find out that Isaac was gone.

'I was by myself when I found out. I became hysterical. I remember that someone I don't know, a woman, was saying you have to be strong for the baby, you have to be strong. I panicked, thinking that by being upset I was going to harm the baby. And so that sort of forced me to shut down emotionally.

'They didn't take me into a room, it was in the corridor and he was on a bed. And I remember just being so shocked when I touched him, he was really cold. And obviously now it makes sense. Back then, it did not. I kept wondering why he was so cold. And he also had this line across his neck that looks like it was cut or something. I didn't know what that was. And I was asking people what's that, but nobody would answer me.

'I read this book afterwards. It's actually by an Australian journalist. And she talks about how people deal with trauma. And there's this whole chapter on how, when you bury or see the body of a loved one, it's really important, particularly if they've died in dramatic ways, it's really important that you're prepared. But there was none of that for me.'

Sarah paused.

It was very hard for me to have an emotional connection with her through a computer screen, but I could still see how much she was suffering despite all the processing and work she'd done on her pain. Sarah and her husband had been seeing therapists for almost two years.

'I always did his bedtime routine with him. I would sing to him "Twinkle, Twinkle Little Star". I'm not very good at singing.'

She laughed for the first time.

'He was starting to learn the words as well. He would sing along with me. And then I say to him that I love him, that his daddy loves him. We're always here for him. And we're just outside if he needs us. I would tell him I love you to the moon and back.

'I did the same routine with him, on that hospital bed next to the morgue. I sang some "Twinkle, Twinkle Little Star" and then I said the exact same things that I would say to him each night. I just started crying uncontrollably, everyone just grabbed me and took me away. I didn't even have a say, they just took me.'

Sarah's voice broke again.

'Seeing him there reminded me of the night he was born. I was in the hospital with him. That night was one of the longest and toughest nights of my life. But it was eventually amazing. I remember that just a few hours afterwards, he was taken to the nursery for some reason. And I remember sitting in the hospital room. I heard a baby crying and there were babies crying all day. But I remember very distinctly hearing this baby crying and thinking that's Isaac. Seconds later, the nurse brings him to his crib. He was less than twenty-four hours old and I could pick out his cry from all the other babies crying in the hospital. We had an instant connection.

'The voice that I still hear now is not that, the one that lingers is not that, it is the one of him crying after the explosion. It's a cry I had never heard before. He was in so much pain, so confused. I cannot forget.'

She sighed. I felt a weight bearing down on my chest. I cannot imagine being in her shoes.

After Isaac's death, Sarah never went back to her apartment or even to the city. She and her husband immediately moved back to Australia.

Two months after the explosion, baby Ethan was born.

'They looked very similar. When Ethan was born, he was an absolute mirror image of Isaac. It was very confusing for me, the most mind-boggling thing ever. They were similar in many ways. And now when Ethan does something that Isaac used to do, it's both beautiful because Isaac lives in him but it is also really sad, it's a reminder that he is not here. I feel guilty because I can't appreciate Ethan for who he is. I am trying and he is very much loved but it is not the same as when I watched Isaac develop, which was pure joy. Everything is tainted with grief.'

It must be so difficult to nurture a new child when you are still grieving for another. I don't know how Sarah did it. What happens if one gets lost in their grief?

'Ethan is saving me. Ethan is one of the reasons I'm still standing. I don't ever want to feel like he's holding me back from dealing with my grief. But you know, if I need to be present for him, I can't be a mess in the corner, crying and rocking back and forth, which is what you feel like doing some days. It's just not possible to just really sit in it. Because you have to be present. I have lost so much, I can't lose Ethan too. But it's hard, I am exhausted.'

The Covid pandemic helped Sarah delay being with other people and their children. But now that life had returned to normal, it was more difficult for her to run away from the reality of other children around and the feelings it triggered.

'I think one of the things that I find hard is that so many of my friends had kids at the same time as I had Isaac. I just can't see them anymore, because they have kids who are the exact same age as Isaac. I just can't face seeing them. They are turning four, Isaac turned four this month. And so being around four-year-olds, I just can't handle that. Later this year, he would be gone longer than he was with us and that's going to be a whole different type of grief.'

I asked Sarah if she felt like a mother of two.

'One of the hardest things, especially when I'm out with Ethan, is people asking me how many children I have. It kills me inside if I have to lie, and just say I've got one child. But if I tell the truth, I automatically start crying. And when it's a lady at the supermarket,

I don't really want to cry in front of lady at the supermarket. So, it's a constant battle in my head, do I tell the truth or do I lie? Either way I end up feeling terrible because I either end up crying in front of a stranger or end up feeling like I have betrayed Isaac. I'm still trying to figure out how to deal with that.

'Isaac made me a mother. He will always be my firstborn. I will always be a mother of two. But how do you parent a child after they are dead?

'My husband and I made a decision right at the very start that Isaac would always be part of our lives, no matter what. Isaac is everywhere in our house, there are pictures of him everywhere. Before we go to bed, Ethan goes and waves good night to Isaac. He doesn't know how to say his own name yet. But he says Isaac. I make sure to include Isaac in all traditions and events to show that he is still with us. We have not celebrated Christmas in two years, but I like to sew. I am sewing Christmas stockings, one for Ethan and one for Isaac. When we are ready to have Christmas, Isaac will have Christmas stockings. I have also bought him Christmas gifts each year since he was gone and I will continue to do that. He used to love to read and it was our special time together. I bought him a book each year.'

Sarah was also fighting for justice for Isaac. She knew the Lebanese judiciary was fraught with political interference and so she joined the families of other victims in their effort to put pressure at the international level. As Isaac also had German and American nationality, authorities in Germany opened an investigation into his death, and Sarah and her husband also joined a lawsuit in the United States. Other Lebanese families didn't have that option.

'When all of this first happened, I remember very clearly saying to Craig, you know, we're never going to see justice for this, it's never going to happen. Let's not waste our energy. It doesn't work like that in Lebanon and it doesn't work like that in most places around the world. But if by chance, Isaac can still see what's going on, I want him to know that I've done everything that I can to fight for him. And for me, if, at the very least, people who are responsible for this, know Isaac's name and face, then that's something.'

So many of the victims' families have not been able to grieve properly because of the lack of justice. They want to see those who killed their loved ones on trial before they can mourn their loved ones, before they can accept their loss.

In our last conversation before the publication of this book, Sarah shared with me some personal news she had not yet shared with the public in a blog. She was 28 weeks pregnant expecting her third child and it was also a boy. She seemed emotional and overwhelmed.

'The day Isaac died was also when I was 28 weeks. So, it's been a stressful period. We only intended to have two children . . . But we decided after Isaac passed away that we would have another child. My husband and I both had siblings and we did not want Ethan to be a single child. He is not of course, he has Isaac, but he would grow up lonely.'

Would a brother for Ethan give Sarah solace? Would it ease her pain? I didn't know what it's like to lose a young child. It scared me to death.

But was Sarah afraid of anything after losing Isaac? Wasn't that her greatest fear and loss?

She told me again and again that fear still lived inside her, it did not leave her. It was all kind of fears. The fear of never being happy again, the fear of losing Ethan, but also the fear of losing Isaac again.

'I am terrified that as each day passes Isaac becomes more of a memory than reality and that my memories will start to fade,' wrote Sarah, . . . 'There is the fear that the pain, which feels like my only connection to Isaac, will fade.'

Sarah gave birth to Baby Levi in August 2022.

LEILA BARAMAKIAN

'He was afraid of cockroaches and ants. Now I go to the cemetery and I see cockroaches all around, it breaks me.

'Look you can still see the blood, they cleaned the tiles over and over again but the blood marks are still there.' Leila showed me the living-room floor where her son Jack lay dead on 4 August 2020. The blood was fading in colour, now looking like pale orange spots, but a year on it had not disappeared, resisting time as if in an attempt to keep reminding her of the tragedy of that hapless day.

Leila was not in Beirut that summer. She was in Jordan visiting her other son and taking care of her grandchildren. Like many Lebanese mothers, most of her children had emigrated. One was in Jordan, another was working in the United Arab Emirates. Jack was the only son she had left in Beirut.

'My other son came from Dubai and saw his corpse. He told me he couldn't forget how his head was half gone, half empty. Apparently, he was standing by the window, the pressure threw him away to one side of the room, his fiancée to the other. He died at home.'

Seven people died in Leila's building including her son, his fiancée, and a pregnant woman. The street where she lived, known as Rabbat Street, directly faces the port.

'He was already dead when they found him. Forty-five minutes had gone before they got to him. If they had found him earlier and found an ambulance earlier, he could have made it maybe.'

Leila and I were sitting on plastic chairs in her quasi-empty apartment. An NGO had helped her rebuild it, but she had not moved back in yet. She was spending a lot of time in Jordan.

She looked for Jack's photos in her phone.

'I look at them every day, I cannot stop. It hurts me but it helps me too because I see him. I even have one of him in the tuxedo when they put him in the box, his head wrapped with a bandage,' she tells me, showing me a photo of him in his coffin.

As she scrolled down the pictures on her phone, I saw a photo of a woman who looked like her. She had make-up, and looked plumper and younger. 'Is that you Leila?' I asked her.

'Yes, it is. My niece told me I looked young before Jacko died.
Now, I look like an old lady.'

Leila was 61. But grief had taken its toll on her. She looked
pale and fragile. The dark pockets under her eyes told me she was
sleepless. Her hands wouldn't stop shaking.

'I protected him for so many years and they still managed to kill
him. I used to breastfeed him in the shelter during the civil war. It
was 1989 and he was just 10 months old.'

Jack was born during the last years of the Lebanese civil war.
It was a period known as the 'war of elimination'. Back then, the
Lebanese forces, a far-right Christian party which is still in power,
was at war with the former Lebanese president, Michel Aoun,
who was then the army commander and head of one of two rival
Lebanese governments.

'I remember spending the nights moving my legs to make sure
that no cockroaches or rats would come to him. I used to embrace
him in the shelter and move my hands and legs so nothing would
come. I often put him in a portable bathtub with a blanket because
I worried so much about insects getting to him.'

Leila sobbed. I hugged her.

'I saw him on the funeral day, I made them open the coffin,
he was so cold. I wanted to move him, to shake him, maybe he
was still alive. I wish I had moved him, maybe he would have
woken up.'

Her phone rang as she was speaking. It was her daughter-in-law.
She told her not to stay home alone.

'I am happy here, I am sitting with Jacko on the balcony, I am
fine,' she replied.

But she was not fine. Leila looked disturbingly agitated and
depressed. I asked her if she was getting any help. She said she
couldn't find her anti-depressants anymore and had to stop them.
She didn't have any long-term therapy. A psychiatrist had just put
her on drugs, but now with Lebanon's crisis in medical provision,
even those were not available.

'He was afraid of cockroaches and ants. Now I go to the cemetery and I see cockroaches all around, it breaks me.'

Leila covered her teary eyes, swinging her head left and right.

'It is not easy to see cockroaches sleeping next to your son and you can't do anything about it.'

She was fixated on the cemetery throughout our meeting. I wondered if it was a manifestation of her grief. It was all she talked about.

'I called the guy in charge of the cemetery and told him I wanted to build him an insulator. My son hated insects. I'll pay everything I have. I will deny myself food and water to clean his burial place and protect it from insects. I asked the Armenian Church to help me fix it, but they have not done anything.'

Leila paused. She looked out of breath. It was a hot July day and her apartment felt like a furnace. Her sister got us some bottles of water.

'I miss him. The minute I wake up, I see him, then I realize he is not there. My other kids tell me to stop crying. To be strong for my grandkids. Why can't I just grieve? Why? Let me be. The first time we went to the cemetery I resisted crying just so I can be there for my other two kids who were crying. We were alone and I was worried something would happen to them because of how sad they were. I resisted crying but I was dying on the inside. I told them let's imagine he travelled. I didn't believe a word I was saying.'

Leila had not stopped crying. She was wearing a black shirt, black pants, and black tights in the heat of the summer, and she had a pin with the photo of Jack on her chest.

'It makes me feel like he is here.'

She looked at the pin and kissed it. She also had a huge poster of Jack hanging on the balcony.

'I clean the poster every day. I just did before you came.'

Leila picked up her phone again and played a video of her son's 28th birthday. She kissed the screen. Jack had white hair and a white beard despite his young age. He seemed jolly.

'When my other children hug me, thinking they could replace him, I feel him, I smell him. I hate it when they embrace me but I don't tell them. I smell Jacko in their hands, in their body.'

She paused and wept.

'I need 15 hundred dollars as a down payment to fix the cemetery. Is that possible? I don't even have dollars. No one has dollars. How will I pay for that? I want to put marble tiles, now there is sand. I want to protect him from the cockroaches. I want to put a frame with his photo so his burial site is easily recognizable. I want to go there and be able to see him.'

When I visited Leila again a year later, she had still not been able to fix her son's cemetery. She said the Church had made empty promises and she had no means to do it herself. Jack had been his mother's support. He was working in a bank in Beirut and had provided for his mother. Leila's husband died years ago after battling a disease. He had been disabled for more than a decade and spent most of his time in bed. She had to work as an assistant in a laboratory to feed her children and take care of him. She was not educated and was married early, at 16.

'It was not easy. I did it all by myself. The two eldest were in school. I would wake up, take them to school at 6.45 a.m., then come back home to Jacko. He was a few months old. He would still be asleep. I would change him, feed him, and take him with me to work. I would leave our door open so that my neighbours would check on my husband who was in bed. It was not easy but I miss those days. They were better than today.'

I asked her if she would go back to Jordan where her other son was. She might find some solace with her grandchildren.

'Yes, my son is asking for me. I will go but after I fix Jacko's cemetery. I need to fix the cemetery.'

Would she find peace once she had done that? Leila seemed like she had not even started to grieve. Two years on, she looked exhausted.

'May they burn in hell. May they burn in hell,' she mumbled quietly.

She had lost so much weight and cried all the time. She reminded me so much of my grandmother, who never healed from her wounds. She would tear up every time she told me the story of her husband's death and how she had raised her children all alone. Even decades after the crime, she still cried. She broke my heart as a child. I remembered how helpless I felt sitting by her side seeing her cry. Leila brought back those uncomfortable memories.

Grief never gets lighter, I guess. People just learn how to carry that burden.

Leila played voice notes on her phone. I asked her who that was. She said it was a conversation between her son and his friend right before the explosion. They exchanged messages on the fire and wondered what was going on. I got goosebumps just listening to them. His friend survived.

'Toborni ya Jacko. Toborni,' she uttered.

'Toborni' is a well-known Lebanese expression often used to show someone how dear they are to you, how much you love them. It translates as 'May you bury me.' It means you want to die before them, so you don't have to live without them.

'May you bury me Jacko, may you bury me.'

Only she buried him and he was just 30 years old.

15

Exodus

NOUR AL JALBOUT

*'I also feel like I am displaced. I have no right to
say I am a refugee but I honestly feel like I do not
belong and I was forced to leave.'*

'I am not home, I don't feel like I am home. I don't feel like I can
settle there. The one thing that keeps me going, my motivation,
is actually thinking that this is transition. I think I am fooling
myself because it is not a transition. It's just so hard for me to
accept that I am not going to have kids in Lebanon one day and
raise them there. I feel angry, I feel guilty. There is also hate, a hate
that grows every day when I realize that I cannot see my parents,
I cannot hug them, I cannot kiss them. My dream was to become
financially independent and take care of my parents because of all
they have done for me, and I can't do it. The distance, the time
difference is just so hard. It is hard to stay connected with the
people I love.

'Then, there is this constant feeling of fear that haunts me. I
go to bed worrying I will wake up and something has happened
to them. I wake up worrying something has happened to them.
I worry they might not find fuel for their car, that they might
not be able to find their diabetes medicine. I feel responsible. I

am so far and I feel guilty. My heart is there. Every piece of me is still there.'

We had barely started the interview and Nour J. was crying and I was crying with her. We shared the conflicted and painful feelings of leaving home.

Nour J. and I had known each other years before the explosion. I had met her when we were both involved in political activism at some point in our twenties. She was a member of the youth branch of a political party, the Democratic Renewal Party, and I was the youth leader of the Green Party of Lebanon. Those were days when we still thought we could change Lebanon and build a better version of it for our children.

We reconnected following the explosion after I had seen a video of her on a media outlet. Then, we both moved out of Lebanon. I went to Paris and she went to Boston.

Nour contacted me in the autumn of 2021, telling me she was passing through Paris for a few days. We met over lunch.

We were both part of Lebanon's fifth mass-exodus wave, which had been ongoing for more than four years. The first two waves of migration were in the nineteenth century and the First World War, and the third and fourth waves were after the birth of modern Lebanon in 1943. The last wave was during the 15 years of civil war, which was from 1975–89. Lebanon has always exported its people, the brightest of its citizens. It has always depended on their remittances and contributions. But that model is no longer sustainable.

Since 2019, at least two hundred thousand Lebanese have left the country looking for a safer and better life. Many of them were the country's most educated citizens. They were tired of surviving, of fighting, of living through uncertainty, and they simply wanted opportunities to thrive and and build a stable life for themselves.

For many, including me, it felt like a one-way ticket. Lebanon was no longer a country with a future, a place where we can raise our children, a place where we can dream, where we are citizens, where we are safe.

'I have no right to complain, I am now in a country that respects me, gives me my rights. I am privileged,' Nour J. told me referring to the United States. 'But it doesn't really comfort me, because I look back home and I see what is going on and it hurts.'

Nour J. was an 'emergency physician', known as an ER doctor in the United States. She was working as an ER doctor at the renowned American University of Beirut Medical Centre (AUBMC) in the summer of 2020 and was hoping to stay in the city despite the onset of the economic crisis a year earlier. But the explosion changed everything.

'A week before, the chair of my department called me and asked me if I had plans to leave, as many were. I told her not really, that we were planning to stay for another year and then decide. I came back to Lebanon from the United States in 2019. I was in Baltimore and my husband and I decided to go back. I wanted to give back to the place that made me a doctor. I studied at AUBMC and the ultimate goal was to come back and work there. After the explosion, I thought that I couldn't do it anymore. It was not an easy decision as I knew that I was contributing to the downfall of the health sector, each one of us leaving was triggering that fall.'

Lebanon's hospitals, once the best in the region, were then struggling with human resources as their best specialists were leaving the country. As this book is being written, according to the World Health Organization about 40 per cent of Lebanon's doctors and 30 per cent of its nurses have emigrated since the onset of the crisis.

In the summer of 2022, as my daughter and I were visiting Lebanon, she caught an ear infection. It was a Saturday afternoon and we needed to get her checked urgently. Her former paediatrician was in the United States, and there were no clinics on the weekend. We took her to the emergency department of one of Lebanon's most renowned eye and ear hospitals. To our surprise, the hospital had no power and was completely deserted. There were no specialists on call, no patients. An intern, probably in his early twenties, checked her over.

The emigration of doctors from the country was just a fraction of the massive brain drain which accelerated after the blast. This exodus continued as it became clear that Lebanon's economic recovery wasn't going to happen anytime soon. The departure of the country's brightest and most talented people, including its youth, will have long-term implications for its future outlook.

'The unpredictability of living in Lebanon has always been with me. I lived through the 2005 assassination of Rafik Hariri and what came after. I lived every day with the fear that something will happen. I was always prepared to face something, for bad things, but not of this magnitude.

'I live facing the port. If I was home I would have died for sure. But I was at the hospital that day.

'The ceiling fell, the fire alarms turned on, and I didn't know what happened. I felt weak. The resident doctor told me to tuck, she had this instinct and I did not. The first thing I wanted to do was to call my parents and tell them I was okay. I had to crawl on the floor and picked my phone and ran to the X-ray room because it felt the safest. Two minutes later only, people starting coming in. They had blood on their face, some carrying their eyes, shrapnel in their head, screams, chaos. We did not understand what was going on.

'The only thing that came to my mind was that they killed the head of AUB, don't ask me why. He was very vocal about the uprising and we thought someone targeted him. That was the thought for about an hour. People kept coming, I kept asking what happened and no one knew. Then I stopped asking and focused on work.

'I was in a mode where I wanted to save everyone and it took me a while to realize that this was not going to happen. I asked my colleague to activate mode disaster. A lot of doctors, medical students, came in to help. I had to stand up and scream and give orders. My job was to go from one room to another and make sure that residents did the right job. I felt overwhelmed. I remember this migrant domestic worker. We stitched her head without anaesthesia and she asked me after where she would go. I told her she had to leave.'

Nour cried again. I had no appetite anymore to finish lunch. She had barely eaten.

'I still remember this and I am scared that I did the wrong thing sending her home. Because we didn't scan her head, we did not make sure there was no internal bleeding. We couldn't. We were very overwhelmed, it was chaotic.

'I had to stop people from performing CPRs and direct them to the morgue. The hardest part is giving up on young people.'

Nour was sobbing. I teared up again. We were in a Parisian café next to my apartment. People sitting next to us must have thought we were grieving for someone. We were actually grieving for Lebanon.

'There is always a guilt feeling, the guilt of surviving, of not doing enough. I will not forget the face of parents begging me to do more. It hurts a lot. I felt like I was in a marathon, running and running, but there was no finish line.'

Nour was constantly haunted by the people she treated that day who didn't make it. Their faces never left her, day and night. She had flashbacks about them, and tortured herself again and again about what she could have done differently to save them.

There was so much guilt felt by the women interviewed for this book, and I felt it too.

'The day I left, I hugged baba and told him I was sorry I was leaving him there. I am so sorry I am leaving you, but I have to go.'

My own father cried like a baby the day my daughter Yasma and I left for Paris. I thought he was in denial until that morning when we got to the airport. He called me right before we boarded our flight. I had never heard him cry so much in my life, not even when my grandmother died.

'My relationship with Lebanon is like loving someone who beats you every day. The country abuses you but you love it so much. My dad is a nationalist, we grew up loving Lebanon. My dad had the option to leave and he never did.'

This reminded me of my father. He had studied in Paris for 11 years, but decided to go back to Lebanon even before the end of the civil war. He worked as a surgeon during the conflict, and he started a political movement in my home town after the war to fight the family politics which had killed his father. He faced all kinds of challenges, including threats to his life for simply deciding to go against family clans and run for parliament in 1990, the first post-war elections.

'I wake up every day wondering if I should have stayed. I think I took the right decision, but yes, leaving my parents was the toughest part. You know they are stuck and there is no way out and it makes it harder.

'I also feel like I am displaced. I have no right to say I am a refugee but I honestly feel like I do not belong and I was forced to leave.

'I am angry at the Lebanese people, I am disappointed, and I am less hopeful. I had hope. I am afraid that things are going to get worse. It's not just economic, the freedom that we once knew is fading away. So many people get summoned and questioned for social media posts, activists are being arrested. I also think August 4th exposed a section of the population that has no sense of belonging to Lebanon. We knew that from before but this is now flagrant. Some people feel like they are not concerned by what happened. It's flabbergasting.

'When I left Lebanon, I first felt like it was a healing process, a kind of therapy from someone that I adored but abused me.

'I love Beirut. I think about it every day, even now in Boston, every day. But I needed to leave to heal. A piece of me is broken.

'How did we get here? How could we have changed the course of history? Was violence the solution? Was it wrong to peacefully demonstrate? How are we going to protect the Lebanon that we knew? Is it coming back? I don't think it's coming back. It's a haunting fear. I have a fear that the Lebanon that I know is going to disappear.'

Nour and I stayed in touch over the course of the year. She texted me this right after the 2022 parliamentary elections.

(Tuesday 10 May 2022 – via WhatsApp)

'I was on a 14-hour flight from Dubai to Boston to make it on time to vote. I felt like I was running to the polling station to meet my lover. It felt like a glimpse of hope, a taste of home, a hug from the motherland. Seeing all these young people voting for change. It strikes me again and again how much I love the land and hate the people ruling it. For a second doubting the decision to immigrate but I know it is still the right one. Every vote is a closer step to go back home.

'Alas, not happening anytime soon. Maybe one day . . .'

YASMA MAALOUF (AND I)

'I want to become a singer when I grow up so I can sing a song about Beirut.'

No one leaves home until home is a sweaty voice in your ear
saying –
leave,
run away from me now
I don't know what I've become
but I know that anywhere
is safer than here.'

Warsan Shire, Home

This is our story, my daughter Yasma's and mine.

I hesitated before writing these pages. I wanted this book to be only about other women, those who had not had the opportunity to tell their stories before. I also felt like I had already shared parts of my story throughout these chapters. But, like the other women, I am an intrinsic part of the story of Lebanon, and its recent past. I was a witness to and a survivor of its history and woes, albeit not with the same intensity and misfortune as them.

My daughter Yasma, now six, represents Lebanon's youngest generation of women, one that has unfortunately also known violence. We managed to transmit our trauma to her generation. From my grandmother to my daughter, generations of women have been condemned to live through the same cycle of violence and abuse, again and again.

In February 2021, Yasma and I moved to Paris. She was just four. Yasma grappled with our departure as she was suddenly taken out of her family nest and introduced to a new world that did not include her father or our extended family. My husband never moved with us.

My decision to leave Lebanon, though, was not made overnight. It was a thought that had been brewing in my mind for many years. As a journalist, I could see the abusive elements of my country way before 2019. I knew this was no place to raise a child. And yet, leaving was never an easy decision to make.

The explosion on 4 August 2020 shattered any excuses to stay. I had to get Yasma out to a place of safety. I had to run for her life and mine.

May 2021, excerpt from a conversation with Yasma

> ME: 'Yasma, why did we leave Lebanon?'
> YASMA: 'Because there are a lot of bad guys. Lebnen is not good anymore.'

She called Lebanon 'Lebnen', using the Arabic spelling, even when she was speaking in English. I loved it.

Yasma and I had discussed our departure again and again. It was not easy explaining to her why we left, and it still wasn't. In her mind, Lebanon was taken over by bad buys, and that was actually true.

When the uprising started in 2019, she stopped going to school because of demonstrations and roadblocks. My husband and I took her to protests with us and she asked a lot of questions. I tried to describe to her what was happening using a childish but Manichean interpretation involving good and evil. It was the closest thing to the cartoon movies she watched. Since then, she has referred to Lebanon's leaders as bad guys.

> ME: 'Why is Lebanon not good anymore?'
> YASMA: 'Because the bad guys they want to destroy Lebnen. All they do is steal money from it.'

I smiled. Her childish depiction of Lebanon's reality was actually very accurate.

> YASMA: 'There is a machine in their house. It has a special button that once they press it, they can remove the power from all of the houses at the same time. It's dark, people can't watch TV, they can't use their phones.'

I learned, and continue to learn, from her imagination every single day.

Power cuts were something both Yasma and I had experienced in Lebanon. Whenever we visit home now, mostly in the summers, Yasma is afraid at night when the electricity is out. This is exactly what my childhood looked like. I used to wake up in the middle of the night and seeing that there was no power but only pitch darkness, I would scream my lungs out until my mother woke up and came to light a candle in the dormitory next to my room. Three generations later, that has still not changed.

Yasma, who loves music and singing, even invented a song about the recurrent power cuts.

'There is no electricity, there is no electricity, oh oh oh. Every day, there is no electricity,' she chants every time the power is out.

We laughed when we should be crying.

I got severely poisoned in the summer of 2022 because of food spoiled by power cuts. I sometimes had to use the flashlight of my phone to use the toilet when it's dark. My husband was paying a fortune back home to keep the private generator running. Our electronic appliances were damaged because of power switches all the time.

ME: 'What else did the bad guys do?'
YASMA: 'They did the big boom and people can get hurt in their houses.'

The big boom was what she called the 4 August 2020 explosion.

ME: 'What happened during the big boom?'
YASMA: 'I was at somebody's birthday with Oli [her cousin], then I was coming out of the car with teta [grandma] and she was talking on the phone with Apo [her uncle who lives in the UK], and then suddenly we heard a big boom. I asked what it was. Maybe it was fireworks. They left the fire on maybe. Teta was crying.'

I was surprised that two years on, she still remembered where she was that day and what happened. Yasma was on the outskirts of Beirut on 4 August, luckily. But she heard the massive explosion and saw the aftermath. Our reaction at home was also traumatizing for her. She is an anxious child who is very aware of her environment.
'I don't like the big boom,' she added.
I sighed. I hope she forgets the blast by the time she is an adult.
It comforts me that she is in a secure place now, as much as it breaks my heart to see her miss her dad and our family. She still cries every day asking for her father. The weeks that follow the end of our holidays in Lebanon are the toughest. It is so hard for her to understand why she cannot be with her father, why he could not move with us.

ME: 'Yasma where was the big boom?'
YASMA: 'It was in Beirut. I remember all of the houses were almost destroyed. Glass fell on the floor. Now, my dad is trying to fix the houses, but still, they need a lot of time to be fixed.'

My husband works in glass. He owns and runs one of Lebanon's largest glass-processing factories. Following the blast and working with local NGOs, he helped rebuild, for free, the glass facades and windows of the most vulnerable Lebanese families. We told Yasma when we left for Paris that he was still doing that and it was the reason why he could not move with us. The reality is far from that. His business, though still afloat, is facing all kinds of hurdles because of the economic crisis. He employs more than 100 Lebanese families and leaving overnight is not possible. Exports are keeping the company alive, but he thinks there is no future for his industry amid the rising cost of fuel, constant power cuts, and the financial crisis. The government has never helped industries in Lebanon. Many companies like my husband's had to fight to survive.

He never wanted to leave Lebanon because of his business, which he inherited after his father passed away when he was just 21. He could not just let go of his father's legacy and start anew. He would get upset every time I mentioned emigrating. When the economic situation deteriorated severely at the end of 2019, we had a huge fight. I told him I was applying for jobs abroad and wanted to take Yasma with me. I did not want her to live without her father but I also could not leave her in Lebanon. After the explosion in August 2020, he changed his mind and asked me to take her and leave at any cost.

Hearing the stories of all these grieving mothers who might never find justice for their killed children convinces me every day that I made the right choice. The pain of leaving Lebanon was nothing compared to the pain we experience when we are there. I do not want my daughter to grow up experiencing the endless cycles of violence that I did. I do not want her to think that wars were just a common occurrence every now and then. I do not want her to live in a country where power cuts are a normal state of affairs. There are so many things I thought were normal growing up in Lebanon that should never be considered acceptable. I want Yasma to have an ordinary life, to feel protected as a child and as a woman later on. I want her to thrive in a stable and peaceful environment. Who does not want that for their kids after all?

I did not leave just because of Yasma. My relationship with Lebanon has always been complicated. I constantly navigate between love and hate. Lebanon has been kind to me in part, but that's mainly because I had a privileged life growing up there. On the other hand, I was also in an abusive relationship with my country that was hard to break away from.

Life in Lebanon was an interminable battle. First, as a journalist I was exposed to everything, from corruption to human rights abuses and political paralysis, from war to sectarian violence. Every day brought with it a new injustice and an impetus for me to fight that injustice. I could not live in my own comfortable bubble, reality came knocking on my door every single day. I did not just report on injustice, like other foreign journalists might do. I lived it, it affected me and the ones I loved. It felt too personal and I was just tired of fighting every day. I was ensnared in many struggles. They gave me a purpose but they also drained me. Covering domestic violence, migrant workers abused by their sponsors, child sexual abuse stories – I put my heart into these stories and went beyond my role as a journalist in my attempt to help those I reported on. There were many attempts to silence me or intimidate me.

I also covered conflict and displacement for many years. A big chunk of my career focused on reporting on refugees in Lebanon and the Middle East. Their stories stayed with me, often haunted me.

As a woman, I also fought many battles, including personal ones. It was not easy asserting my personal freedom and choices in a society that was not just traditional and patriarchal but that also denies us our individuality and freedoms for the sake of others: the larger family, the community, and society. As a woman, you have to spend so much time pleasing and impressing others that you end up not really existing as a person. In my own marriage I

had to confront both family and society. I wanted to have a civil
ceremony, but civil marriages are not legal in Lebanon. Couples
have to go abroad to get them. Religious institutions want to
maintain their grip on marriage for many reasons: It's a power play,
for both sectarian and economic purposes. All weddings performed
in the country are religious and registered under the husband's
birth jurisdiction. If a woman marries from another religion, she
has to convert. My husband and I are from the same religion, but
we wanted a civil ceremony at all costs because we believed that
it was a basic human right. I also wanted to protect myself as a
woman from discriminatory religious laws. I had the option of
getting married abroad, but I wanted to do it at home.

In 2013 I covered the story of the first-ever civil marriage held
in Lebanon and registered by the state. With legal support, one
particular couple found an interpretation of the law that allowed
them to have a civil wedding in Lebanon. The law stipulates
that those who do not belong 'administratively' to a religious
community are eligible for a civil marriage. This couple removed
their sects from their family registry, based on a decree issued in
2007 which allows citizens to delete any reference to their religion
in state records. They married through a Lebanese notary and
after a legal battle against the government, the ministry of the
interior recognized their marriage. This unprecedented case stirred
considerable controversy and was decried by religious leaders. At
the same time it encouraged many, including me, to follow suit.
My husband and I removed our religion from official records. I
remember that even my own father, who was secular, resisted my
decision to do so and was worried about what people might say
when I walked in to ask the civil servant in my home town to
remove my sect from my registry. I didn't care. Why does the state
have to know what my religion is anyway?

We married through a notary in 2014. But a new, more religiously
hawkish minister took over the Ministry of the Interior and refused
to recognize our marriage as well as that of about 50 other couples.

We filed a lawsuit against the state, but to no avail. I was eventually forced to obtain a civil marriage in Cyprus after two years of fighting for a recognition of my marriage in Lebanon. I got pregnant with Yasma in 2016 and could not wait anymore. She risked being an undocumented child had we not registered our marriage.

Yasma was born in 2017 in New York. I wanted her to have a foreign passport at all costs. I spent my life applying for visas and worrying about getting rejected because of my Lebanese passport. Giving her an American passport felt like an accomplishment.

Motherhood was something I really wanted but it also had an unexpected impact on my mental health. Early on, I struggled with conflicted emotions. In Lebanon and in our patriarchal Arab world, women are instilled with the idea that motherhood is an inevitable role, a duty, more like a 'raison d'être'. Women are told that motherhood is only beautiful and tender. But that is just half of the story. Motherhood traumatized me as well. I felt so confused in my new role and often resented being a mother. But because those feelings were not socially acceptable and I was raised thinking motherhood was natural, I rebutted or repressed them. It damaged my experience with motherhood at the beginning as I was left feeling guilty all the time. It was not until I started having therapy, two years after Yasma was born, that I made peace with myself.

The year 2018 was a turning point for my mental health. My grandmother Dalal passed away early that year. It was a difficult moment in my life as I was deeply attached to her. Her death also triggered traumas from the past.

I had been sexually molested as a child by someone my parents employed as a driver. This is the first time I have spoken about it publicly, and my own parents will recoil at this news. Although it was a brief incident, or so my memory tells me, it damaged me. At my grandmother's funeral, I saw the man again and the past came back to haunt me. I had been suffering from PTSD and recurrent night terrors, the result of both personal and work-related traumas, and they got considerably worse after that day.

A friend recommended an excellent trauma specialist and I went to see her for the first time in February 2018. I remember crying throughout most of that first session, telling her I was tired of life in Lebanon and all the battles I had to fight. I thought my struggles were just related to Lebanon and its context. In fact, the external environment was just a manifestation of my own internal struggles.

In that first session, I could not speak about my childhood traumas, let alone the sexual molestation episode. Instead, I found refuge in the injustices that happened to other women. I always did.

I remember mentioning to my therapist a recent episode that I found painful and made me angry. I was at a restaurant in a mall and a migrant domestic worker was standing as her employer enjoyed a lavish meal with her friends and kids. I had to intervene on behalf of that woman, stirring a fuss at the restaurant. It was not the first such incident that I witnessed. There was another one before that, in which I was with my whole family and my brother and I made a scene. I always felt helpless in such situations, but also uncomfortable and embarrassed. I was ashamed by our lack of humanity and our indifference. I was also hurting on the inside as a woman.

Therapy challenged me to face my darkest thoughts, including all the traumas from my childhood. The man who had molested me ended up killing himself. It felt like a closure.

Therapy also helped me reconcile with my conflicted feelings, including those I had for Lebanon. It helped me to recognize something I had ignored for so long: the feeling of being trapped in Lebanon. I was feeling as though I was in a giant prison and I could not get out of it. I thought leaving Lebanon meant losing everything, including myself. But that was not true. I loved Lebanon but it also hurt me and wearied me. It was hard living with this sense of a conflicted identity and I did not know what to make of it.

Therapy liberated me. Leaving Lebanon for good became an option, at least in my head. I did not know back then that, three years later, an imminent crisis and an apocalyptic disaster would help me make this brave decision.

Life in Paris has not been easy. Living with a child by myself is demanding and often lonely. I eagerly wait for my husband to come and visit every month. We miss him a lot. I identify with the mothers in this book who raised their children alone. It is a challenging task, even if I am not alone all the time.

But Paris offered me inner peace, a sense of stillness and serenity that I never felt living in Lebanon. Paris also represents freedom, individuality, stability, and human values that I believe in. However, to be honest, it does not feel like home yet. It is not a city where you can fit in easily as a foreigner. I am still waiting to feel at home here.

Lebanon, on the other hand, is and will always be home, despite what it took away from me. In Lebanon are my roots. My story started there. Lebanon is pain, a lot of it, but it is also life and love. It is the backbone of my childhood memories, the bits and pieces of a broken relationship from which I will probably never recover.

It is not easy feeling constantly torn between two places, and not feeling whole in either. Maybe my identity is just that, it is not defined by one place, it is not static or complete yet. I am still forging it.

Excerpt from a conversation with Yasma in August 2022 as we were driving to Beirut's airport after spending the summer in Lebanon

ME: 'Yasma, why are you crying?'
YASMA: 'I want to stay with papa.'
ME: 'He will come visit you soon.'
YASMA: 'My cousins are lucky, they have both their mum and dad with them in Abu Dhabi.'

I didn't know what to say. I was hurting. I told her our separation wouldn't last too long. Soon, we would be together again. I hugged

her. We were sitting in the back of a cab and it was dark outside.
Not a single light was on. Lebanon drowned in darkness.

> YASMA: 'Are we passing by Beirut?'
> ME: 'Yes, why?'
> YASMA: 'Oh no, the houses.'
> ME: 'What?'
> YASMA: 'I don't want to see the destroyed houses.'
> ME: 'It's okay. Not many broken houses are left. They fixed
> many.'
> YASMA: 'Yes I know, but it's hard to fix Lebanon. The fixers of
> the house are trying their best to fix the houses. The problem
> is they can't fix all of it. It's too messed up and it takes a lot of
> days to fix.'

She might have been only six, but she got it all.

> ME: 'You once told me you wanted to become a builder when
> you grow up so you can fix Beirut. Is that still the plan?'
> YASMA: 'I want to help Lebnen and fix it. But I am too small to
> fix it.'
> ME: 'Maybe when you are older?'
> YASMA: 'Actually, I want to become a singer when I grow up so
> I can sing a song about Beirut.'

I smiled.

> ME: 'What will the song be about?'
> YASMA: 'About the explosion. The boom was very strong. It
> collapsed everything. It was a lot of harm. And everybody had
> blood so they died.'
> ME: 'Did you see people with blood?'
> YASMA: 'No, but I see you bringing medicine to Lebanon
> because they are sick. Everytime we come, we need to give
> medicine. We don't want them to be sick and die.'

She was mixing things up. That was normal.

I told her it was not why we had been bringing medicine with us from France. There was no medicine in Lebanon anymore or it was very expensive.

YASMA: 'Yes, also that. They can't find it in Lebnen.'
ME: 'Will you miss Lebanon?'
YASMA: 'I will miss papa and teta, my house and Biscuit [our dog]. I will also miss going to Ehden.'
ME: 'Ehden?'
YASMA: 'Yes the place where my tata [grandmother] goes in the summer.'
ME: 'What is nice about Ehden?'
YASMA: 'There are a lot of flowers and tata has a big garden where we can play.'

Ehden is my home town in the north of Lebanon. I spent all of my summers there. The town is perched over the holy Qadisha valley, a UNESCO heritage site that has sheltered monks for centuries and inspired artists from across the world. Ehden brings up the most vivid childhood memories in me: the chilly mist covering red-tile roofs on August afternoons; the smell of home-grown corn grilled in my grandmother's garden; my siblings and I running speedily past lavender fields in my parents' garden for fear of being stung by a bee; my late maternal grandfather's breakfast tray; the soft aroma of his Turkish coffee and the taste of the small ring-shaped cookies he had with it; afternoons eating Lebanese Kaak, a big loaf of bread with sesame seeds often complemented with unpasteurized goat's cheese and fresh raisins from my grandmother's vineyard; summer nights in the town's busy square meeting friends; clubbing with my girlfriends in the town's discotheque; eating Sahlab, a sweet milk-based Lebanese pudding, following a long night dancing. Ehden is my first summer crush, my paternal grandmother's green swing, and endless starry nights in my parents' garden.

I want Yasma to experience all of that, and it is why I make sure she goes back to Lebanon every summer, at least for now.

> ME: 'Do you like Beirut?'
> YASMA: 'I do but now it's too messy. Everything is broken.'
> ME: 'A lot of people are leaving Lebnen like us. You know it is not just you, right?
> YASMA: 'Yes, it is good.'
> ME: 'Why?'
> YASMA: 'They are smart, they don't want to hurt themselves and die. Beirut is a dangerous place, I don't want papa to stay here.'

This ached a bit. She was maybe too aware of danger and death.

> ME: 'But then no one will be left in Lebanon.'
> YASMA: 'It's a little bad yes, because they need to fix Lebnen, and the fixers who fix the houses cannot fix it alone.'

It is a sad reality and probably an irreversible one. Tens of thousands of Lebanese emigrated in 2021 alone. So many families have been separated over the past three years. I felt guilty choosing the exit door, but for me there was not even a choice. Lebanon was not a place where I could raise Yasma anymore.

I stopped covering Lebanon and the Middle East after we left. I welcomed the opportunity to cover a new beat. Part of it was because I wanted to create some distance, to heal. Another part of me wanted to learn about a new country and report on a new region after more than a decade spent in the Middle East.

But the truth is, I never really disconnected from Lebanon. My family is still there and social media is a daily reminder of home. Working on this book also meant visiting often, keeping up with the country's developments and the lives of women in it. It's often painful because I feel helpless.

Every time I visit, I have bitter-sweet feelings. Nothing is the same anymore. My longing for Lebanon is based on pure nostalgia.

In Paris, and even from a distance, Lebanon still stirs so many emotions in me. It still makes me cry. I grieve for it every single day.

Sometimes I just wish I could unplug myself from Lebanon, forever, but I am not sure I would survive.

16

'Glorious Days' Gone Forever?

COSETTE KHAIRALLAH

*'There was beauty everywhere. I used to love life
and I was very beautiful.'*

Cosette is the woman I met the most throughout my two years working on this book. There is something about her that kept me coming back again and again.

She is the oldest woman in this book. I met her through her granddaughter-in-law, who follows me on social media. I was looking for older women to interview, namely those who had lived through the golden age of Lebanon.

Cosette's nickname is Coco and it suits her well. She is coquettish, always dressed up even when she has nowhere to go. She is the most jubilant 86-year-old woman I have ever met, with so much wisdom but also a passion for life you can rarely find among people her age. We have a great time together. She makes me laugh and leaves me hopeful every time I see her. Coco lives her life as if it is still long. She never makes you feel that she is old and is never passive. She cherishes the little things we take for granted and tells me 'nothing ever spoils her mood'. 'The key to a long life,' she says, 'is crushing the bad feelings before they crush you.' In many ways, she is the opposite of my grandmother, who was not very jolly. Her positivity is a panacea.

However, I think the reason for my attachment to her lies elsewhere. There is something about Coco that satiates me. It is the image she represents, an image of Lebanon I desperately want to cling to, an image we were told represented the pinnacle of Lebanon. Coco is my journey into the glorious days of Beirut, when it was dubbed the 'Paris of the Middle East', my glimpse into the golden 60s, decades I only knew through photos and movies. She is a living representation of a Lebanon that is no more, probably gone forever but one that I want to keep close to my heart.

Coco was a young woman amid the best days of Lebanon. From the 1950s to 1975, and despite the war in 1958, Lebanon witnessed its most glorious days, an age of prosperity and cultural renaissance.

Back then, Lebanon's growing banking institutions driven by a laissez-faire attitude and a bank secrecy law, attracted Arab capital mostly from oil countries in the Gulf. Beirut beckoned the jet set. Wealthy tourists flocked from around the world and celebrities such as Brigitte Bardot and Omar Sharif frequented the city's fashionable bars and nightclubs. Louis Armstrong played jazz in Beirut. The city was a safe haven for political activists and artists from not just the Middle East, but all around the world. There was freedom in Lebanon in the 60s like nowhere else in the region. It was a social, economic and political freedom that we no longer have today.

Remembering the 60s does not mean I am purely romanticizing that period. I understand that these years were never sustainable and much of that glitz and glamour was really just a myth. In reality, the 1950s marked the birth of an unsustainable system that would later fail. These were also the years where economic inequalities started increasing, and the seeds of antagonisms and the 1975 conflict were being planted. These glorious days masked a reality that would soon surface.

Coco was born in 1936 to a middle-class Beiruti family. She was a pioneer in her career and was the face on postcards celebrating the wonders of Lebanon.

First, I want to tell you that although I met Coco in 2020, I had actually known her all my life. Coco was the face of a famous advertisement from my childhood. It looks like a very sexist ad now, but we grew up with that TV spot, imitated Coco, and loved her as children. In the advertisement, she walks into a small shop in a total panic asking an old man, known as Abou Fouad, to help her as she is swamped with cleaning chores. She says her in-laws invited people over to dinner and she had to make them proud. Abou Fouad gives her an all-purpose, made-in-Lebanon cleaning product. At the end of the advertisement, her mother-in-law praises the cleanliness of the house and Coco's husband raves about her as a housewife.

Ironically, Coco was never just a housewife. She was married and had two children but worked throughout her life and had a successful career in marketing when most women did not really work.

'I used to promote sanitary pads in schools. I was the first woman to enter a school and train on sanitary pads. I used to go train girls how to use the pads. There was a lot of resistance from the schools at the beginning, but I persisted and convinced Catholic schools to let me in to educate the students. I had 900 girls to train as early as nine years. It was very delicate because back then they would mix feminine hygiene with sex and I didn't want to sound like I was there for sex education. I managed the campaign and I went in very traditional areas.

'I was promoted to sales supervisor. I got to know everyone, schools, pharmacies, convents.'

We usually met at her apartment in Achrafieh in Beirut. It was in a 1960s all-concrete white building with a terrace overlooking a tiny street. Coco was always sitting there sipping her coffee. Her apartment was damaged during the explosion but luckily she was not wounded.

'The house was never destroyed the way it was destroyed on 4 August. Not even during the war. Once a mortar fell on my room. There was a hole in the ceiling but that's it. What I saw during this blast is unprecedented.'

But I wanted to talk to Coco about the good old days. I was here for that.

She asked me to help her snatch a casting, she wanted to be in advertisements again. I laughed but she was serious. I made a few calls but to no avail. It was only a year later, that a casting agent called her back. Coco got a role in a music video with the Lebanese and Arab pop star Nancy Ajram. She was so proud of herself and it made me so happy.

'I was the postcard face of Lebanon,' she tells me. 'There is a postcard of me holding a basket of fruits, it was taken on the terrace of the Phoenicia hotel.'

She stood up and brought over a copy of the postcard. Coco was wearing a beige fishnet shirt, holding a giant fruit platter and biting on an apple with a smile.

The Phoenicia hotel as well as the Saint George hotel were both symbols of Beirut's 'dolce vita'. The luxurious five-star hotels, hanging over the city's prominent bay, once known as Saint George Bay, beckoned wealthy tourists from all over the world.

'You would find the most beautiful women in the world basking in the sun at the Saint George beach club. They would wear the trendiest bikinis and sip cocktails. It was the first and most famous beach club in Beirut.'

The Saint George hotel was damaged during the war and has still not been rebuilt because of a legal land dispute between its owners and the construction giant Solidere, which is affiliated to the late prime minister, Rafik Hariri. The hotel now lies deserted with a giant poster that says 'Stop Solidere'. The Phoenicia hotel closed its doors after the Beirut blast and only reopened at the end of 2022.

'There were also regular fashion shows at Saint George's club. I used to go watch models on the runway, they came from around the world. In the seventies, I worked in sales for Jack Kassia, a famous designer from Latakia in Syria. He had a shop in rue de Phenicie next to Saint George. People from Cannes came to buy his dresses. That year, it was 1971, Georgina Rizk was elected Miss Universe, she was representing Lebanon. She used to come to the boutique and I used to dress her up. Arab princesses were also our customers.'

I envied Coco for having lived through that. Beirut was still a bustling cosmopolitan place when I was growing up, but this was something else, on another level.

'Rue de Phenicie boasted the best nightclubs in the region, I remember the Epi Club and Les Caves du Roy, probably the most exclusive of them. I never went there as I could not afford it, but I heard that famous people were there all the time. Beirut witnessed an influx of foreign money and investment in the 1950s. It was the mother of the world, a source of culture and an education hub. There were students from the Arab region who came here just to study at the American University of Beirut. Arabs came here for hospitality, for the weather.'

Coco's family was never rich but unlike today the middle class in Lebanon were thriving and had a good life.

'In the summer, we used to rent small tents by the Saint Simon public beach in Beirut and spend our days there for almost nothing.'

The Saint Simon beach, once a pristine shore, is now a strip of illegally constructed and crammed concrete buildings with trash all around. Beirut's only remaining public beach is the Ramle bayda, but even there sewage runs straight into the sea and a resort has been illegally erected by the shore.

Private resorts have mushroomed and encroached illegally on public beaches in Lebanon since the civil war. They charge hefty prices and are inaccessible to most Lebanese.

I asked Coco about the cultural scene. Beirut was still a city of art, music, and literature, but nothing like before.

'Burj Square had so many movie theatres, very big ones, I used to go there with my sister. There were Lebanese and Egyptian movies. It was our favourite getaway. We had cotton candy, popcorn, and watched movies with Faten Hamama, Ismail Yasin [Egyptian actors], and Sabah [Lebanese actor and singer].'

Burj Square is now known as Martyr's Square and is surrounded by a giant parking lot and office buildings.

'We also went to watch Chouchou's show at Piccadilly in Hamra,' she added, referring to the late Lebanese actor and comedian Hassan Alaa Eddine, known as Chouchou, who founded the national theatre. Piccadilly's theatre was a landmark of Lebanon's golden age; Dalida once sang on its stage. The theatre has been closed for more than 28 years and caught fire in 2000. Recently, the Ministry of Culture announced its renovation but that was still pending funding.

Coco also got to know Lebanon's most famous singer, the one and only Feiruz.

'I went to watch her perform as a kid. She was not married and had still not known the Rahbani brothers. She had a song called My Butterfly, I remember telling my mother that she was going to become Lebanon's finest vocalist and she did. Then in the 1950s and 1960s, I made it in her choir and participated to the Baalbek International Festival. The festival attracted princes from the gulf, famous artists. After the festival, people would wait for us to greet us. One time, at the end of the show, I was chosen to give a flower bouquet to the Algerian president, Habib Bourguiba. So many important people came to the festival. We would stay there for 18 days and were accommodated at the famous Palmyra hotel, at the expense of the government.'

The Baalbek International Festival was created in 1956. It's an annual summer festival that has been hosting local and renowned world artists for decades. Acclaimed musicians like Miles Davis, jazz singer Ella Fitzgerald, French singer Johnny Hallyday, and Charles Aznavour and others performed under the majestic Roman ruins of the Temple of Jupiter. Unfortunately, the festival was suspended during the civil war and has faced major setbacks since because of political instability. Today, and despite the crisis in the country, the festival is fighting to survive and is adamant about being a prominent cultural form of resistance.

'I used to be in Sabah's choir too, I used to imitate her all the time,' she added.

Coco stood up and sang. She was wearing a tight cotton purple dress with a pink bra. She was always so fashionable.

'Oh Lebanon, you mean the world to me. I had wished to live a lifetime in your embrace. Loving my country is the best song I have in my heart, it's a treasure. God bless Lebanon, the heaven of our dreams . . .'

I smiled. She was a real performer and could still put on a show even after so many years.

'There was beauty everywhere. I used to love life and I was very beautiful.'

Coco grinned proudly, a flashy orange lipstick highlighting her thin lips and contrasting with her short white hair.

'My husband was an engineer at Middle East Airlines, I used to have free tickets to fly around the world, I spent my life travelling. But my husband had to leave his job at the airport during the civil war because they killed his cousin at a checkpoint near the airport. And it's been a downfall since and I stopped travelling so much.'

Every time I visited Coco, she asked me about Paris. As much as she was my vessel back in time, I was hers. There was so much longing for the past in our conversations. Even the civil war, said Coco, was better than the situation today.

'We lived a good life from nothing, a modest life. As a woman, I lived well, I was a rebel, I drove a motorbike. People used to wait and see what I wore when I went out. I was happy, I made money. Now you don't make money anymore, they just take it away from you.'

Coco took me to her bedroom to show me her collection of vintage hats. There were tens of them in all shapes and colours. We tried them on and laughed. I bought her a lawn-green scarf from Paris. She loved it.

'I used to travel a lot but always looked forward to coming back here. I love Lebanon, it has my heart. My son has been in the United States for 36 years. He always wanted to give me a Green Card to live there, I said no. This year I told him I would take it. I can't work anymore, and I have no pension fund. If you see Macron [the French president], he is the only leader who came here after the explosion, if you see him, tell him Cosette wants French citizenship.'

We both laughed.

'I am happy you are here, you made me forget my pain. I am happy you are here and listening to me.'

I felt the same towards her. Coco was my happy pill.

'It's a dead end, the banks took my money, I cannot work anymore. I am not famous anymore to do ads. I have no pension and no savings. I spend my time playing the piano and singing and I also go walking.

'Beirut has changed a lot. But you still feel attached, nostalgic, you remember where you used to go out, where your parents' house was, you long to see those places. You long for that freedom. We now know our golden days were bound to be short-lived. I wonder if any of it was even real. But nothing is like what we are living today. Today is the worst of all days.

'It's too late for me. I have no time left to wait. I cannot give anymore. I need to take. I gave everything I had, now I am tired and I need people to look after me and help me.'

If Lebanon were to speak, I thought to myself, it would utter similar words.

Afterword

I was asked once what it would take for me to go back to live in Lebanon. My answer is simple: accountability. Not economic recovery. Lebanon's problem lies in its governance, it is not economic but political. Once that is addressed, then getting out of the crisis is possible. Accountability doesn't mean peace in the Middle East, which is beyond our control as a tiny nation, although I would like to see Lebanon standing aside from regional conflicts. I would also want Hezbollah to be disarmed and prevented from jeopardizing Lebanon's search for peace. How that can be achieved is another question. I still want to believe that the solution can come from within, through a Lebanese dialogue within Lebanon's borders.

What I certainly want is simple. It is for us, as people of Lebanon, to have the ability to hold those in power, those who commit crimes, those who strip us of our rights, those who let the country collapse, liable.

I cannot raise my child in Lebanon if I cannot punish those who have the ability to harm her, those who yield power to deny her rights.

Rights are violated everywhere around the world, but accountability lies in a nation's ability to punish those who violate them, including the powerful. As a mother, I want to make sure I can protect my child.

All of the women in this book are victims of impunity. And history keeps repeating itself in Lebanon because of that impunity. From my grandmother, whose husband was killed in 1957, to my daughter Yasma, who survived the Beirut explosion in 2020, one of the largest non-nuclear explosions in history, those in power keep perpetuating violence in various forms and in different contexts. Along with the violence comes, always, impunity. Rinse, repeat!

As this book was written in early 2023, no progress had been made in the Beirut blast probe, leaving the women interviewed here in a state of limbo, demanding a justice that is elusive. Politicians in power are doing everything they can to avoid any liability and erase the last trace of their crime. Those accused of blowing up my city, Beirut, are roaming free – they are still in power.

In the meantime, at least six women were killed in systemic family violence in 2022, including Hanaa Khodr, a 21-year-old mother of two who was burnt alive by her husband. No one was held accountable. Domestic violence is on the rise amid the economic crisis gripping the country, according to human rights' organizations.

Migrant workers continue to be enslaved and abused under the kafala system. Women still cannot pass on their nationality to their kids. They still have unequal rights in courts.

The state of individual freedoms has never been worse. During the four-year term of the former president, Michel Aoun, 801 freedom violations were reported, according to the Samir Kassir Foundation for the Freedom of the Press. Lebanese journalists and activists, including women, are still being summoned, arrested, and questioned by the anti-cybercrime bureau for social media posts, merely for publishing their opinions or for speaking out. A famous Lebanese comedian, Shaden Fakih, was accused in June 2022 of 'insulting security forces' in a joke she made and posted online during the pandemic lockdown. In a farcical call, she asked the government electronic platform for permission to leave her house to buy sanitary pads. Shaden was questioned and fined. But those responsible for blowing up an entire city were not. Those accused of killing women and raping girls were not.

We want justice and it is not only justice for women. It is justice for depositors who lost their lifetime savings, justice for victims of the explosion, justice for victims of the civil war that ended in 1990, justice for victims of the bombings, justice for the disappeared, justice for the misery and daily humiliation we have to endure.

There will never be healing, reconciliation with the past, and peace without justice. Every Lebanese is seeking justice today.

When I decided to work on this book, I had a few objectives in mind. First, I wanted to give some of the victims and their families a safe place to tell their stories in detail, so they are known to the world and not forgotten. I also wanted Lebanon's women, the marginalized actors of my country, to write their own history. This book is by women and for women.

But mostly, my objective was to document my country's unprecedented collapse through the voice of its people, the most vulnerable and the bravest, especially in the absence of work on collective memory and oral history in Lebanon. Our shared memory is crucial for any process of reconciliation, truth, and justice. It is vital in order to rebuild Lebanon one day.

The process of meeting these women and writing this book also helped me process my own trauma and feelings about the Beirut explosion. It made me realize that so many shared my pain. It also immortalized our stories when Lebanon's politicians want them expunged. It somehow made me feel less guilty about leaving Lebanon. It felt like I was still fighting for it, from a distance.

I am no therapist but I know that many of the women in the book never had the chance to speak openly, without any filter, about their stories and their pain. It gives me some peace to know that I might have helped them, one way or another, by simply lending an ear. Ultimately, I feel very privileged to have got to know these women, some of them closely, and to hear them tell stories that often they have never had the opportunity to speak about before. It wasn't an easy journey for any of us. Being in my seat might seem like a privilege but it also came at a cost. Hearing all these stories, sometimes for hours, witnessing the pain and not being able to do much, often left me feeling uncomfortable and distressed. I conducted most of the interviews in the summer and autumn of 2021. I suffered from insomnia for many months after and that was partly due to the work I did with them.

The Lebanese women you read about have suffered a lot and many of them continue to suffer to this day. They are victims and survivors of a system that keeps alienating them. They are bearing the largest brunt of today's unprecedented crisis in my home country without any official safety nets. But their courage and defiance are also extraordinary. I take strength from them every single day.

Acknowledgements

So many people believed in me and in this project, and it is thanks to them that this book became a reality. I want to thank my agent Doug Young from Pew Literary. Doug committed to this book even before I had finished the proposal, while his guidance and constructive feedback took this project to the next level. It is because of him that I landed on Bloomsbury as a publisher and worked with the amazing Tomasz Hoskins and the brilliant Fahmida Ahmed. Thank you both for believing in the power of this book, for your patience and generous time. I also want to thank my copy-editor Richard Mason for his meticulous work on the book.

There are many women to whom I am forever grateful. First and foremost is Sarah El Deeb, a stellar AP journalist whom I proudly call my friend and who helped me shape this project from beginning to end and took the time to read the text and edit it. I want to thank Julie Tegho, an outstanding oral historian who encouraged me to write this book and helped me with the historical context. I also wish to thank Carmen Geha, a friend and long-time activist who took the time to offer valuable suggestions on some chapters.

A big thanks go to Nour Sleiman, who helped me transcribe all the women's interviews. I also want to thank the lawyer Marise Doueihi for walking me through the details of women's personal-status laws in Lebanon, and economic consultant Danielle Hatem for editing my timeline. I am also grateful to Hind Darwish, an award-winning editor, for taking the time to read the book before it was even edited.

I also owe thanks to my father, Kayssar Mawad, who helped me with Lebanon's complicated history and guided me through the historical chapters in this book. He is also my inspiration in many ways. I want to thank my mentor and former professor, Nawaf Salam, a judge at the International Court of Justice and a writer, who was among the first people to know about this book and who dedicated his precious time to editing my introduction. A special shout-out goes to my husband Ibrahim Maalouf, who is my greatest support system. Last but not least, the biggest acknowledgement goes to the women in this book. Thank you for opening up to me, for trusting in me, for spending hours telling me your stories, and for sharing your pain with me. I am honoured to have known you. I hope you find peace and justice one day.

How To Help

Part of the author's proceeds will go towards helping the women in this book. If you wish to support any of the women in this book, please contact me: dalalmawad@gmail.com

A list of trustworthy local non-governmental organizations that you can donate to:

1) Education
   Krystel El Adm Foundation
   https://krysteleladmfoundation.org

2) Reconstruction and Relief
   Offre Joie
   https://offrejoie.org
   Bayt el Baraka
   https://beitelbaraka.org
   Together Li Beirut
   https://www.instagram.com/togetherlibeirut/?hl=en

3) Medical Support
   Donner Sans Compter
   https://www.dsclebanon.org/en
   Med Donations
   https://www.instagram.com/medonations/?hl=en
   The Lebanese Red Cross
   https://www.redcross.org.lb

4) Mental Health
   Embrace
   https://embracelebanon.org

5) Migrant workers
   ARM
   https://armlebanon.org
   Egna Legna
   http://contact.egnalegna.org/lebanon

6) Refugees
   Amel https://amel.org
   Basmeh & Zeitooneh
   https://www.basmeh-zeitooneh.org
   Sawa for Development and Aid
   http://www.sdaid.org/

Index